# Wrestling Hurricanes

# Rave Reviews for
## Wrestling Hurricanes

A compelling story of faith, courage, and perseverance of how one woman battled her storms by following Jesus. Tiffany doesn't just crack open the door of her drama, she throws it wide open and invites us in to learn from her remarkable journey through adversity. Buy two copies of her book . . . one for yourself and another for a friend. We all need the kind of encouragement that she gives us in *Wrestling Hurricanes.*

**Dennis Rainey,**
co-founder of FamilyLife and "FamilyLife Today"

Ms. Haines writes in a way that few of her contemporaries have yet to capture. *Wrestling Hurricanes* enlightens the mind, inflames the heart, and engages the will. That is why it is not only a map into the peaceful eye of the hurricane but also a truly life-changing experience, a book to reread as well as give away . . . Ms. Haines writes in a manner that embraces all our *common experiences*, out of her own personal *weaknesses*, and therefore *Wrestling Hurricanes* is a good book, indeed even a great book.

**—Dr. Barry R. Leventhal,**
distinguished senior professor,
Southern Evangelical Seminary and
**Mary P. Leventhal,**
leader of women's church ministries

*Wrestling Hurricanes* is a beautifully written personal story of the author and her family wrestling hurricanes of unbearable physical and emotional pain. I was moved by her extraordinary determination to overcome the waves upon waves of trauma afflicting her —as a strong-willed mother—her children, her marriage, and her faith. This book will inspire, bring answers, and give renewed faith to parents of children with emotional struggles and women dealing with cancer.

**—Lana Bethune,**
family advocate and wife of Ed Bethune,
former member of House of Representatives

Sometimes God uses simple lessons to show us the way. Other times, the journey is much more complex and arduous. No matter what challenges we face—large or small—God has a plan and a purpose for our lives. One cannot read Tiffany's soulful account of her and her family's storm-filled life without coming away transformed by the power and mercy of God's abiding love for us. Tiffany shows us God not only meets us where we are, but He walks with us when we can no longer stand.

—**Dave and Barbara Zerfoss**,
authors of *Stress is a Choice* and
*Stress Less and Enjoy Each Day*

What a story! This is a page-turner. I sense this book is written to help parents dealing with PANS and their children. But it is so much more. "God uses our mess as our message," and He has certainly done that with Tiffany's life. I highly recommend this book. Parents who have children with challenging issues need to read it. Breast cancer victims need to read it. People who suffer with running and other similar obsessions need to read it. There is so much to be revealed in this book. I never knew that that this cute, quirky, fun little girl that I've known all her life had so much grit!

—**Dixie Fraley Keller,**
author and speaker

This book is so amazing! Having several PANS grandchildren, I know what it's like to watch helpless as this crazy brain inflammation causes so much pain and trauma. Doctors and researchers need to read this book. Tiffany has truly shown how we all push forward to do it our way, and God waits for us to let Him guide us! "It's not about me!" I love how she pulls it all together, showing her vulnerability, how it has strengthened their marriage, and how it's taught her and her family that Jesus is enough, even when answers are few. I have been privileged to read her story. It needs to go viral.

**—Judi Gertz,**
grandmother of PANS kids

# Wrestling HURRICANES

## Navigating Life's
## Relentless Storms
## for God's Glory

# TIFFANY HAINES

NASHVILLE

NEW YORK • LONDON • MELBOURNE • VANCOUVER

# Wrestling Hurricanes

## Navigating Life's Relentless Storms for God's Glory

Published in New York, New York, by Morgan James Publishing. Morgan James is a trademark of Morgan James, LLC. www.MorganJamesPublishing.com

ISBN 9781631953057 paperback
ISBN 9781631953064 eBook
Library of Congress Control Number: 2020944513

**Cover Design by:**
Rachel Lopez
www.r2cdesign.com

**Interior Design by:**
Christopher Kirk
www.GFSstudio.com

Morgan James is a proud partner of Habitat for Humanity Peninsula and Greater Williamsburg. Partners in building since 2006.

Get involved today! Visit
MorganJamesPublishing.com/giving-back

*To the mission, the essence,*
*and the fulfillment of the Glory of God.*

# Contents

Acknowledgments . . . . . . . . . . . . . . . . . . . . . . . . . . xiii
Foreword . . . . . . . . . . . . . . . . . . . . . . . . . . . . . . . .xvii

**Prelude** . . . . . . . . . . . . . . . . . . . . . . . . . . . . . . . xxi

**Part I** . . . . . . . . . . . . . . . . . . . . . . . . . . . . . . . . . .1
Chapter 1 | The Calm Before the Storm . . . . . . . . . . . .3
Chapter 2 | The First Eye Wall Hits . . . . . . . . . . . . . .17
Chapter 3 | It's Not About Me . . . . . . . . . . . . . . . . . .29
Chapter 4 | Survive and Advance . . . . . . . . . . . . . . . .37
Chapter 5 | The Deluge. . . . . . . . . . . . . . . . . . . . . . .49
Chapter 6 | Fight For Your Marriage . . . . . . . . . . . . .57

**Interlude** . . . . . . . . . . . . . . . . . . . . . . . . . . . . . . .67

**Part II** . . . . . . . . . . . . . . . . . . . . . . . . . . . . . . . . .73

Chapter 7 | The "-ectomy" of Me. . . . . . . . . . . . . . . .75

Chapter 8 | The Lightning Strike . . . . . . . . . . . . . . .91

Chapter 9 | PANS and the Problem of Pain . . . . . . .107

Chapter 10 | Kate . . . . . . . . . . . . . . . . . . . . . . . . . . .117

Chapter 11| Understanding the Eternal Weight

of Glory . . . . . . . . . . . . . . . . . . . . . . .123

**Postlude**. . . . . . . . . . . . . . . . . . . . . . . . . . . . . . . .133

A Note about PANS and PANDAS . . . . . . . . . . . . .137

Open Letters. . . . . . . . . . . . . . . . . . . . . . . . . . . . . .139

About the Author . . . . . . . . . . . . . . . . . . . . . . . . . .149

# Acknowledgments

I want to start off by thanking God for unveiling the concept that it's not about me. It wholeheartedly changed my life to understand that it is all about God's glory. God beautifully changed my perspective and relieved the pressure that I must carry the weight of the world. God's glory tips the scales in a profoundly fulfilling picture that shapes my life's purpose.

Brad, this book exists because you are committed to truth and seeking truth. You have loved me tirelessly beyond anything I could have ever dreamed. I do not deserve your faithfulness, and yet everyday, you heap blessings upon me. You are my best friend. You are my favorite person and embody every joy I find on this broken earth. You make life fun and meaningful and happy. You are long suffering, patient, and incredibly kind. "I love you" doesn't cover the fraction of its depth.

I want to thank my family. Mom and Dad, you have provided spiritual depth and knowledge of the Bible that is invaluable. So many years ago, both of you left your homes and followed Jesus. Not a religion but Jesus. You taught me how to be more like Jesus. Not judge, not follow a church protocol, but simply love Jesus. Your thirst for studying the Bible made me find joy in its pursuit. Mom, this book exists because you exist. My sisters and brother—Kathryn, Carmen, and Todd. You are my best friends. I don't laugh with anyone like I laugh with you. You have cried with me and loved me and supported me. You are my favorite people to be with on the whole earth. Kathryn, thank you for understanding and bonding with Kate. She has been profoundly loved by you.

I want to thank my in-laws, John and Linda Haines, and my brothers- and sisters-in-law for loving and supporting us. PANS has ravaged so many in our family.

I want to thank my Auburn college friends, Julie, Eugenia, Paige, Laura, and Sarah (even though you graduated from UVA). You have loved me faithfully. You have loved me like Jesus. You are the one I turn to for prayer every time I'm in crisis, which is a lot. Thank you for laughing with me. Thank you for supporting me. Thank you for not judging me when there was much to judge. Thank you for making life fun and adventurous and more like heaven. I love you.

I want to thank my neighbors. You have loved us, supported us and held us up when we were most discouraged. You have accepted us without condition. You have loved Kate so faithfully and fully. You see her beauty and never expected her to fit in a defined box. We are eternally grateful for your friendships.

Thank you Max Lucado, C.S. Lewis, and John Maisel for writing books that helped guide my understanding of the fact it's not about me, and it's all about God's glory. Thank you for your logic and expertise in explaining this deep concept that changed the entire framework by which I view life.

Thank you JC Konecny for giving a name to the darkness we all have experienced. God has used you in so many people's lives. Thank you Jessica Gavin (founder of PRAI, Pediatric Research and Advocacy Initiative), my PANS friends, and the PANS community. When I'm enduring my darkest days, you are there for me. You understand me better than anyone. You stay up late at night helping others through their pain, understanding the trauma that lies in its wake. Thank you.

Thank you, PANS. PANS is difficult to thank but is in fact necessary. Thank you for teaching me what true evil is and the lies that it embodies. Thank you for bringing me to my knees and perching me on the edge of the moral frontier. Without you I would never see my fragility and darkness within. Because of you I see God, light, heaven and GLORY. Thank God you have been defeated and destroyed and burned into dust. I'm thankful Glory has replaced your filth and weighs infinitely more.

Thank you to Cortney Donelson. I can assure you that without you, this book definitely doesn't exist. Your patience, love, and experience were the perfect match to this message. God handpicked you to write this book with me. Thank you for listening to God's call to put people's stories on paper for God's glory.

Thank you to Morgan James Publishing. Your willingness to take a chance on an unknown, unproven writer is beyond appreciated. I pray you are blessed for allowing me to be part of your writing family. Thank you for your ingenuity and creativity. Thank you.

# Foreword

God's ways certainly are not our ways. The path God chose for my daughter would not have been my choice, nor hers. But God knows something about each of us that we don't even know ourselves. His path is right, though it may be difficult. His path leads us to give Him glory. He can have it no other way.

Little did I know that fifteen years ago when I first heard a message titled, "The Glory of God," (by John Maisel), it would be a catalyst that would change the course of my life and that of my dear daughter. For some odd reason, after I had been a Christian since childhood and been in ministry for several decades, I had never heard a message that had such an impact on me personally. The man who gave this message had been one of my husband's dearest, long-time friends. The effect on our lives was profound.

At about the same time, God was also doing a work, unknown to me or even to Tiffany, which would alter the course of her life and the life of her husband and family. Tiffany and Brad had been married a number of years, had three precious but difficult children, and all the while, God was relentlessly being the Hound of Heaven, pursuing them with one of the highest callings anyone could perceive. He was imprinting on their hearts "the glory of God" message, not only for them but for countless others who would watch their lives and listen to their story.

One day, Tiffany called me to tell me that she and Brad had been learning about God's order and that we were created for His glory. This idea was radically changing their perspective. I remember giving them John Maisel's message and with that message, this book was born. Tiffany would go on to teach, counsel, share, and live out this amazing message to whomever God put in her path. She has taught this concept to her children, her neighbors, and her friends—anyone who will listen.

Tiffany and Brad "got it" in a way that is understandable to us common people. Neither are theologians, so they wanted to communicate this message in a way that a child could understand it. Their lives have been "turned right side up" through understanding the glory of God as our endgame. It is the answer to all our questions, both great and small. It is the answer to the "whys" of life. It gives us the answer to why it's not about us. It's all about Him and His glory.

It has been a joy to watch, from a mother's viewpoint, the growth and maturity of a child whose heart is sold out to our heavenly Father. I know you will be amazed as you read their story.

In love,

Sally Meredith, co-author of *2 Becoming One*

# Prelude

n the following pages, as I unravel my struggles, I pose a question: What would happen if we knew there was one concept, one key, one answer that explained why we are here—our purpose? What if this same answer would explain every tragedy, every storm, and every dilemma while equally explaining every triumph and joy? What if our children were taught this concept from an early age? How would our lives—their lives—be different? What if I told you what I'm about to share through my life story is the most important thing you might ever learn?

It's the *Big Idea*. It's God's strategic objective for mankind. This concept is simply **the Glory of God.**

*"The deepest passion of the heart of Jesus was not the saving of men, but the Glory of God; and then the saving of men, because that is for the Glory of God."*
—G. Campbell Morgan

"The Glory of God is the framework for all life. It gives us the answer to the 'whys' of life. We may not understand the mystery of how events will work out, but it shows us how *everything* is being leveraged for His glory and why this is so important. It explains why some people appear to be successful, while some appear to fail time after time. It explains why some have strong athletic bodies and others struggle with health or weak bodies. It helps us understand when God hands us a sweet cup to drink from and when He hands us a bitter cup," as John Maisel from East West Ministries says.

We can take comfort in this truth: God's glory and our individual stories—whether they include full-blown hurricane seasons or trials by fire—are for the future Kingdom of Heaven. 1 Peter 5:1–2 says, "Therefore I exhort the elders among you, as your fellow elder and

> The deepest passion of the heart of Jesus was not the saving of men, but the Glory of God; and then the saving of men, because that is for the Glory of God.
>
> —G. Campbell Morgan

witness of the sufferings of Christ, and a partaker also of the glory that is to be revealed, shepherd the flock of God among you..."

This is an incredible call! We have been chosen by our Heavenly Father to suffer so that others may gain our knowledge. Our compassion. Our love, which we learned by partaking in the sufferings of Christ. That's the highest call—the highest job—and one that provides the greatest joy. You see, your desire for perfect kids, a perfect spouse, a white picket fence, and a life trimmed with all the money, wealth, and health this world can buy pales in comparison with the call God has given us.

C.S. Lewis says, "It would seem that Our Lord finds our desires not too strong, but too weak. We are half-hearted creatures, fooling about with drink and sex and ambition when infinite joy is offered us, like an ignorant child who wants to go on making mud pies in a slum because he cannot imagine what is meant by the offer of a holiday at the sea. We are far too easily pleased."

As you read, open yourself to hear what God has to say to your heart. I hope by the end of *Wrestling Hurricanes*, you will have grasped what I believe is the truth of all truths, the concept of all concepts, and the beginning and the end of why we are here. It is the most important truth we will ever learn.

# Part I

*"No man knows how bad he is
till he has tried very hard to be good."*
—C.S. Lewis

# CHAPTER 1

## The Calm Before the Storm

Hurricanes are large, swirling storms with winds clocking seventy-four miles-per-hour or higher. That's faster than a cheetah—the fastest animal on land. In our country, we have advanced warning and communication systems for imminent hurricanes. We're aware of their approach days, sometimes weeks in advance. In many countries, communication systems are not set up to reach much of the population. In outlying mountainous areas, rural villages, and remote coastal regions, hurricanes are seemingly born out of the bluest skies and grayest-green waters, the only indicators being a line of spiraling clouds on the horizon and increasingly treacherous ocean currents first noticed by the local fishermen. At that point, it's too late.

I never really questioned my childhood blessings. I always assumed life was good because I followed the "script." There was no trauma, no crisis. I never perched on the margins of moral or emotional meltdowns, even as a teenager. I had several areas of anxiety and stress as a child, but there was a certain ease to everything I did, and I attributed all this to my ability to play by the rules. I concluded that my safe and easy life was the result of my ability to be—and do—good.

I walked through adolescence as if I could do no wrong, as if I could control the world with all its swirling circumstances, because I believed I did. At least it seemed that way. My formative years were mostly quiet and chaos-free, a time when things seemed calm, much like the silence before an argument or the ease before the difficulty—the lull before a storm.

I was a top student, a star athlete, and a church-attending kind of girl. From birth to my mid-twenties, I lived in what I now know explicitly as the calm before the storm.

If you're familiar with the Enneagram Assessment, according to the Enneagram Institute, I am "The Helper." I am *that* person who will bend in twelve different directions to comfort or serve others through their struggles, even if it means giving up my own needs or ignoring self-care.

Growing up in the Washington D.C. area, I was the youngest of four children. Adventurous. Spontaneous. Talkative. If I had taken the Enneagram Assessment in high school, I would have likely been categorized as "The Enthusiast," otherwise known as "The Entertainer." I loved life and wanted to squeeze as much out of it as possible. While I didn't participate in the rebellious activity that so many of the other teenagers—my peers—experimented with, I certainly accepted all the behaviors that went on around me. I was compassionate and had many friends, but I never identified with them per say.

I not only loved life; I was loved. I grew up in a Christian home, and while I may not have always felt like I fit in, I definitely belonged. A religious-infused logic reigned in my world. I tackled most of my decisions and lived my life through the lens of the formula, "If A, then B."

*If I am a good Christian, then I'll have a good life. If I'm obedient, life will be easy.* At age ten, while singing "Amazing Grace" in church and listening to the words—particularly "that saved a wretch like me"—I thought, "This song isn't about me." I was sure the words just didn't apply to me. I was a good girl, never in trouble, and for the most part, obeyed by parents and loved my siblings. *I was no wretch!* Years later, I would come to a very different realization. I think God implants memories in us for later use. He uses a past realization for future teaching.

There existed a dichotomy, though. As a young child, I lived in perpetual anxiety. On the surface, what looked easy wasn't as easy as everyone assumed. Through the eighth grade, I battled the symptoms of anxiety and OCD (obsessive-compulsive disorder), worrying constantly. My siblings teased me, and I was the brunt of many of their jokes. They didn't understand me because they were much more laid back than me. I'm sure my siblings just didn't know what to do with me, and their jokes were never meant to harm me. My reaction to all the teasing is interesting to me now. I didn't cry or complain about it, never running to Mom or Dad like so many other children who are more inclined to tattletale. I fought for my position. My siblings, without knowing so at the time, made me tough.

I chose the "no pain, no gain" mentality and even though my anxiety oftentimes rendered me feeling debilitated, I decided to overcome it rather than wallow in it. This is the code I continued to live by for decades to come. I became a unifier, a peacemaker, and a planner. Since I was often the odd one out, I used humor to mask my pain. Despite my anxiety, I did whatever I needed to do to feel accepted by my fearless siblings. I say "feel" accepted, because today as I look back, I realize they did accept me as they knew me. Unfortunately, no one knew my anxiety rumbled just below the surface of my jokes and positive outlook. This "no pain, no gain" transformation was my way of fighting to be a part of the narrative of our family.

My parents taught us to talk through conflict. There were no brushing uncomfortable conversations under the rug in my home. My parents were in full time ministry most of my life starting churches and various other ministries. Most notably, they wrote a book called *2 Becoming One* and continue to run their marriage ministry called Christian Family Life today. We were taught a "marriage" language from birth which taught us to openly discuss problems within the family. We were praised for our character, not our accomplishments. Looking back, I realize my parents truly mirrored Jesus. They didn't teach me the "If A then B" mantra. Yet I still learned to believe, "If I'm a good person, God will bless me." As a society, we lean toward this belief. It's a lie.

In Genesis 3, Satan convinced us (through Adam and Eve) of the lie that we can take things into our own hands. The world, since then, has accepted this. It works. And then it doesn't. When it doesn't, we don't seem to know what to do with life when we do *A*, and *B* doesn't follow. This experience either drives people toward God or away from Him. For those who believe in God, it's very difficult to experience struggles and have our relationship with God remain unchanged. Whether we run to God or run from God, it's a false premise. Even following God is hard and filled with struggle.

While my parents cared for my relational health (I felt valued, heard, and respected), my anxiety was never specifically validated or treated. Around this time, I started running track. It became an outlet for my stress.

My track coaches subscribed to the "no pain, no gain" philosophy too. Our coach believed in the "there's no crying in baseball" mantra. My will to defeat the narrative was apparent even then as I went "all out" and threw up after every race. This mantra also gave me permission to keep running while stuffing my anxiety down into the depths of my soul as I strove to be "good." It also influenced my decision to ignore the nagging pain in my hip.

\*\*\*

Sixth grade was a defining moment for me. I only call it a defining moment because I am constantly rewinding my memories to revisit these circumstances I'm about to share. I had never been bullied, but at the age of twelve, I joined the middle school track team. One particular boy on the team and I bonded, and we became good friends. I'll call him James.

The problem started when other female track athletes decided I shouldn't be so friendly with James. It turned into the middle school cliché we see on TV shows and read in fiction books. One of these female track members—

whom I'll call Angela—rammed me into the lockers and verbally threatened me. I was confident and well accepted at the time, which prevented me from fearing her threats.

One day, I shared my Angela experience with my older sister, an eighth grader at the time, and she went into "sibling protection mode" and wanted to confront Angela.

"No. Let me try something else first," I begged her. "I'm going to kill this girl with kindness."

So, every day, Angela whispered something horrible in my ear as we passed in the halls. And every day, I responded with a compliment.

"Angela, you look beautiful today."

"I love your outfit."

"Angela, you ran such a great race today!"

This went on until one day, I found myself alone, face-to-face with Angela in the locker room after PE (Physical Education) class. The rest of the class had already walked out, and we were somehow last in line together. True to a Hollywood drama, instead of following everyone else out, Angela turned and with outstretched hands, slammed me into the lockers.

"I'm going to beat you up," she snarled.

I looked her straight in the eyes.

"And you would totally win," I calmly replied. It was the truth. I was much smaller than Angela, and she was angry. But strangely, I remained unafraid. She ended up storming out of the locker room doors.

After that day, Angela must have decided I wasn't worth the effort since she couldn't get under my skin. The bullying ended.

Months later, Angela approached me in the school cafeteria.

"Can I talk to you?" she asked, nodding to a corner of the room.

My friends urged me not to go with her.

"I'll be fine," I told them.

When we reached a place where no other student might eavesdrop, Angela turned and looked *me* in the eyes this time.

"I'm sorry. I shouldn't have treated you the way I did. You're actually a really nice person."

We ended up becoming friends, and that was that.

When I think about this kind of unlikely redemption between two girls who were so different, I realize maybe God was planting a seed.

The Angela story is one of the ways God gave me pieces of truth to tuck away for my future. This seed grew into the knowledge that we are all the same on the inside. He wanted me to remember we all have permission to grow and change. He was showing me that in many ways I *was* like everyone else, capable and living in sliding doors, open to all types of sin. Angela wanted to fight. **Most people want a fight when fighting seems easier than the alternative**—feeling the rejection, abandonment, vulnerability, humility, grief, and hurt of this world. Yes, Angela wanted to fight, but what she really wanted was to be loved. Just like you. Just like me.

***

High school was fun, as most teenagers think it should be. I had a lot of friends at school, and I loved my youth group at church. My "entertainer" tendencies began to thrive during this time in life. I was adventurous, fun, outgoing, and always the life of the party. I never felt like I needed to drink alcohol to fit in. I was confident, bold, and wasn't afraid to be a Christian in a rebellious world.

Ironically, I felt happier with people who didn't always play by the rules. This was in opposition of my childhood where I felt more comfortable coloring and associating myself within the lines. I somehow felt more akin to "sinners." My youth group relationships started to fade as I began spending more and more time with the "partiers." I continued to do the "right things," however, thinking this would lead to more blessings.

However, a dichotomy existed within my soul. Why did I identify more with "sinners" than with "church goers?"

During this time in life, my anxiety seemed to disappear,

> Why did I identify more with "sinners" than with "church goers"?

only appearing in fleeting moments. I loved this version of Tiffany. Maybe it was only a brief moment in time where I was relaxed enough to see I was more comfortable with "sinners" because I was in fact just that. Furthermore, this was also the first time I felt "judged" by church friends. Why did I feel happier and safer with people who accepted me no matter how good I was? Why didn't I feel accepted in church where I was supposed to feel that way?

After high school, I attended Auburn University (in my opinion the best college in America). War Eagle!!! After high school, I grew tired of the "party" scene and was anxious for friends who identified with my love of Jesus (minus the judgment). "Sinners" who loved Jesus. Looking back, I was trying to balance my childhood full of rule-following perfection with my fun-loving teenage years. I met a group of friends whom I'm still incredibly close with today. They have stuck with me through thick and thin. They have never judged me, even through my questioning and despair. They are truly examples of what Christians should be. They recognize their sin in its entirety. They don't gloss over it and they own and accept it, knowing Jesus died for it. For this reason, they never shunned me, but have loved me tirelessly.

I ended up living with my first roommate for all four years. She is still one of my best friends today. I was messy, happy, and enjoyed every minute of college. We had a group of friends that satisfied my every "enthusiast" need. Brad, my future husband, was part of that group, but we were only friends for most of college. We went on multiple spontaneous road trips, attended Auburn football games all over the Southeast, and talked endlessly for hours every day. We watched "Friends" and "Seinfeld." Life was, in every way, fun.

During college, my faith deepened dramatically. Time is abundant in college, and I was able to have meaningful prayer times. I often realized and proclaimed how much I loved Jesus. This time, it wasn't because I was supposed to or ordered to by a religion or its directives. It was genuine, deep, and brought me incredible peace. For the first time, I saw Jesus from a lens that wasn't about rules or judgment. I saw him from a pure depth of innate knowledge of how much He loved me. On one occasion, I asked Him to teach me, *at all costs*, how to glorify Him in everything I do. I didn't have any idea what that meant at the time. I didn't know the darkness that would have to come in order to achieve that end. There was no trepidation in that request. I didn't know the battle that would rage just a few short years away.

In his book, *My Utmost for His Highest*, Oswald Chambers wrote, "In the process of sanctification, the Spirit of God will strip me down until there is nothing left but myself, and that is the place of death. Am I willing to have no friends, no father, no brother, and no self-interest—simply to be ready for death?" Was the term, "at all costs" something I was ready for? It wasn't possible to understand what I had just asked God for. I certainly didn't understand what "dying to self" meant.

Throughout most of our college years, Brad dated a good friend of mine. Months after they broke up, God opened both Brad's and my eyes to our love for each other; it was much more than just a friendship sort of love. My friend could have chosen the road of hate and resentment. Instead, she chose to look at Jesus. She mirrored Him, reflected Him, and gave both of us considerable grace. The same grace God had given us on the cross. I love her and she loves me. We are still friends today.

Brad was accepted to dental school in New Orleans, and we got married shortly thereafter. Life was great. It felt just like a fairy tale at the time. Everything was going just as I planned. My "If A, then B" mantra was right on schedule. What could go wrong?

During the first three years of our marriage, intermittent gray clouds appeared, but I didn't feel any glaring threats. I had been suddenly thrust into providing for two people while Brad was in dental school. My sister was backpacking in Europe with one of my best friends while I was working fifty-five-hour weeks as a C.P.A. Brad was constantly stressed in dental school. Perhaps it was a nugget of envy. I missed the carefree life I had enjoyed in college. We loved our friends and had fun, but I was starting to feel that something was brewing. I didn't know if it was from within or something external. I assumed it was that life was becoming harder, that the reality of adult life was setting in.

Brad graduated and I found out I was pregnant. For a moment, all was well with the world again. Brad was hired by an existing dental practice in Huntersville, NC. I would be back in town with my sister, Kathryn, with whom I'm very close, as well as my parents and my brother. I remember holding Brad's hand while peering into the beautiful blue sky the day I found out I was pregnant. It's easy to give God glory when everything seems to be going our way.

Little did I know that on the horizon, the gray swirls of a hurricane turned, barreling toward our seemingly predictable, wonderful little life. Even though my spirit had been talking to me, telling me something was amiss, there were no overt storm warnings and no reports urging us to take cover or seek higher ground. Sometimes, that's how storms come—suddenly, violently, and relentlessly.

# CHAPTER 2

## The First Eye Wall Hits

know the Tiffany Haines who existed before December 3, 2001, but she doesn't know me. That day changed me. Truth be told, the nine months leading up to that day was when I felt the initial effects of the first hurricane in my life.

Because of my somewhat easy childhood, my expectation was that my life would remain tranquil. I anticipated living in *that* house, the one with the manicured lawn where giggling children skipped over the flowerbeds and not through them. I expected a peaceful marriage with Brad, one in which nothing would stress our relationship to its breaking point. I desired the pursuits of happiness, health, and success. There had been no reason for me to anticipate anything other than what my younger self had experienced.

The thing about expectations is that they are so fragile. Much like glass vases, if you hold onto them too hard, they can shatter in a moment's time, leaving shards that pierce and shred the fingers of those who are left to clean them up.

At nearly the point of our baby's conception, I succumbed to a migraine of nausea. Hyperemesis gravidarum. It's a complicated medical term for a condition characterized by stark nausea, vomiting, weight loss, and electrolyte disturbance. Mine was severe.

By severe, I mean I was throwing up twenty to thirty times per day. I couldn't work. I couldn't even cry without triggering the symptoms. I was often debilitated, feeling chained to my bed or the bathroom. I had become emaciated, weighing only ninety-nine pounds at twenty weeks pregnant.

A category two hurricane had planted itself right in the middle of my perfect little life during my first pregnancy. Then 9/11 happened. Along with the rest of the country, I mourned, and my emotional state worsened. My pregnancy—though I didn't think it was possible—became even more stressful. For three months, it felt like the whole country couldn't function without being sad. I was no different.

The eye wall of a hurricane is a ring-shaped area of especially strong convection surrounding the eye. It is the strongest part of the storm where the top winds reign. December 3, 2001 was the day our first child was born. We named her Kate. The eye wall of this hurricane was upon us. If people had warned me what that day (now over eighteen years ago) and the following days, months, and years would bring, I would never have believed them.

The day Kate was born, I had an infection. After twenty-four hours of labor, the hospital staff rushed us in for an emergency C-section. Much like my pregnancy, her birth proved to be stressful. With Brad's medical background he was fully aware of how my life was in the balance because of an extreme amount of blood loss. Leaving the delivery room, he and the doctors were traumatized. My doctor reminded me the next day of her concern that I could have died during delivery.

The manner in which Kate entered the world would be indicative of her life to date. She went directly into the NICU. Because of my infection, I wasn't permitted to see her for nearly three days. That's an extended period of time to miss during the initial mother-child bonding period—the attachment process. She needed me, and I wasn't there. It threw me into postpartum depression. I felt separated from her at the beginning, and it's a feeling that would continue for years.

Our new daughter wasn't faring so well either. She often turned blue, hyperventilating for more air. The doctors attached several diagnoses to her and assured us she would be fine. Upon our discharge from the hospital a week later, one of the nurses said goodbye with these words, "Good luck. She's got some lungs on her."

For the first six weeks, I experienced repeated trauma as a new mom. My childhood anxiety resurfaced. There were times when I entered our infant's room, looked in her crib, and discovered she was blue again. She had a swallow disorder and wasn't nursing, never drinking more than two ounces at a time. No one was sleeping. As with a wild animal who can't be tamed, I couldn't look my daughter in the eye. She was constantly sick, miserable, and tormented. On some level, I blamed myself. My mom came over in the middle of the night on countless occasions to help, because it was all too much to handle.

Kate never simply cried. She screamed. When we changed her diaper or her clothes, she wailed as if she was being tortured. We kept dressing her in warm, fuzzy sleepers, wondering if she was too cold or not comfortable, but we would have to disrobe her when her screaming wouldn't stop. What we didn't know and learned much later is that she is highly sensitive to certain materials, sounds, and other stimuli. Among a dozen other diagnoses, Kate has a sensory processing disorder.

We had to drive Kate around in the car in the middle of the night. It was the only thing that seemed to calm her enough so she could fall asleep. My mom took on this chore many times. We were so grateful for her help.

At four months old, Kate was diagnosed with "failure to thrive." Failure. To. Thrive. Those words cut me to the core. My anxiety spilled over, and the doctor said something, which looking back, I know was more harmful to my emotional state than she intended or either of us ever realized.

"You need to be on medication. You have an anxiety problem." Her doctor not only didn't believe how bad our situation was, but completely dismissed my concerns. Oftentimes parents of children with health issues feel judged when they need to be listened to.

Throughout my life, I had battled anxiety, and it never really dissipated as an adult. Most of the time, it nestled itself just below the surface so not many people knew about my struggle. It was obvious to me, though, since none of my siblings battled this particular demon. My fiercely competitive nature took those anxious feelings and morphed them into the mindset of, "I will just have to overcome this." But now, a doctor seemed to be blaming at least a portion of my daughter's health on my anxiety. It was gut-wrenching, especially for an overachiever who had never failed before. Guilt joined my anxiety and tormented me.

Up until this point in my life, everything I had done was categorized as successful. Now a parent for the first time and battling through my child's health struggles, my own doubts, and generalized anxiety, I came to the awful conclusion that I was a failure for the first time in my life. And it wasn't just with regards to parenting.

Brad had met and fell in love with a fun go-getter in college. Since I hadn't built any close friendships in our new town, and with our parenting journey going the way it was, the Tiffany he knew slipped away. He had only seen glimpses of anxious Tiffany. I had kept her so well hidden. So, our marriage struggled for a time with the trauma and broken expectations we both experienced. Brad had just started in a new dental practice, his staff wasn't adjusting well to a new "boss," and 9/11 had ravaged our country. I was struggling everyday with the reality that now my fun "adventurer" self was a distant memory.

Life was hard, not what I expected, and I started playing the blame game. I felt like Brad's life *must* be easier than mine. After all, I was an extrovert and loved being around people. He was around people all day, while I was trapped at home with a miserable screaming baby. I was miserable and Brad was my target. One day, he came home and after one of my long daily rants exclaiming how great his life was and how horrible mine was, he yelled out, "I don't even want to come home anymore!"

This became a crossroads moment for me. We all have moments in time when we come to a fork in the road. I will mention several in this book. But that day, instead of retaliating, I relented. I realized that day that I wouldn't want to come home either. Brad wasn't the problem.

At six months old, Kate suffered a reaction to a vaccination and ended up in the Emergency Room. Her tiny leg was swollen and blue. There was a lack of oxygen and blood flow in her leg. Her pulse was 200. They immediately gave her medicine to calm the swelling and lower her pulse. This event catalyzed eighteen months of illness and hospital visits. She was constantly sick. Sinus infection after sinus infection, constant stomach pain, chronic diarrhea, and constant screaming. One day, she had a 105-fever, and her eyes rolled back in her head. She had pneumonia and was rushed back to the ER. Her tiny body housed several different strains of strep in her bloodstream. She had a compromised immune system and was very sick. Sepsis in babies usually does not end well. For nine long days, she lay in the hospital with tubes coming in and out of her body. Finally, the blood culture showed which antibiotics she needed to reverse the condition. She was finally discharged, but we were all left traumatized.

Through all of this, I watched other new moms around me as their children learned how to sleep through the night, breastfeed, enjoy healthy lives, and even ride in car seats without screaming, and I completely fell apart. Living as a parent of a child with health crises is a very lonely place. It's not culturally acceptable to think, let alone admit, that we don't like parenting when parenting is so tough. I felt the pressure to make everything right. Make it good. Of course, I had no control, but that just made me feel worse. I couldn't do anything to change my baby's struggles or our chaotic household.

The overachiever in me asked, "What have I done wrong?"

Because I believed the way I viewed and interacted with God influenced my circumstances, I continued to seek Him daily. Sometimes hourly. I knew the simple fact that during trials, we either move toward God or distance ourselves from Him. I didn't want to slip away from His grip. I had learned growing up that accomplishments were not as significant as character, but "accomplish" and "move" was all I could think to do. I praised Him throughout the day. I listened only to Christian music. I prayed harder for God to fix her. I couldn't just sit and let God be God. I prayed more because I wanted God to bless us. Looking back, it was all about me. Meaning, all I was focused on was going back to my carefree life where suffering wasn't part of the narrative. I wanted the happy life I thought was the epitome of happiness. Little did I know that when C.S. Lewis wrote our "desires not too strong but too weak," he was talking to me, to you.

He has a much more fulfilling happiness prepared for me, a "vacation by the sea," as C.S. Lewis says. He wanted us to realize that His plan involves helping others. I was not ready for this message yet.

Confusion enveloped me as I wrestled with disappointments and unmet expectations. Why aren't my obedience and praises met with less heartache? Why is my world still so dark? "Why is she still so sick? What is happening?" Much like someone staring down the eye wall of a major hurricane, I lived in desperation as I watched everything around me fall apart, not realizing until ten years later that no amount of faith-based achievement was going to change what was happening.

Within raging storms, there are sometimes moments of calm, times when the world finds itself bathed in fresh air, and the lushness of the landscape, caused by the rains, appears beautiful rather than ravaged. The problem is that the damage is still evident and the storm is still there. Everyone knows the brokenness, barrenness, and sometimes, bitterness of what was lost—the cost of braving the storm—will resurface. It's a moment of reprieve before the winds and rains return to wreak havoc once again.

After that long string of hospitalizations, there was a brief time when Brad

> Why aren't my obedience and praises met with less heartache? Why is my world still so dark?

and I were able to catch glimpses of the person Kate could be. Her fun personality started to break through despite the ongoing health issues. Her language was advanced. But I knew something was wrong. The doctors were just as confused as me because she had obvious developmental delays but was speaking in complete sentences by eighteen months old. However, they only knew to mark progress with certain visible milestones.

"She'll be fine. She walked late, but she's walking. She's speaking on time."

My concerns were dismissed, but I still knew in my soul that something else was going on. Kate interacted fairly well with other kids, but her odd behaviors and extreme anxiety isolated her and prevented her from participating in typical social or school functions, such as playgroups. And there were some behaviors I just couldn't explain. Despite the lack of answers, Brad and I discussed adding another child to our family. We had always wanted a big family.

My hyperemesis gravidarum was not as bad with my next pregnancy, but at times, I was still debilitated and struggled with weight loss. The most difficult aspect of the second pregnancy was Kate's chronic sinus infections and continued challenges, including night terrors. Kate literally never slept. I don't use the term *literally* in a flippant way. She would only sleep for an hour or two at a time. We were exhausted.

It was during this season, I learned for the first time there would be no doctor who could help us. There was even an argument of sorts with one of the pediatricians.

"Our daughter's infections are not improving with antibiotics," I told her.

"There is no way she still has a sinus infection, the doctor said. Her sinus cavity is not yet developed!"

Our daughter was three years old at the time, but I requested a CAT scan. The radiologist confirmed she had the worst sinus infection he had ever seen in a child her age. The pediatrician ended up apologizing, but this began my career as a researcher and advocate for my daughter. Somewhere in my gut, I knew no one would fight for my child like I would.

A surgeon finally removed our daughter's adenoids to relieve the string of sinus infections. This experience fueled my need to do what was good, what was needed, and what was right to help my child. My controlling tendencies were now fully evident, and I was ready to take control. I wanted to be smart—smart enough to fight against doctors' opinions if warranted.

What I forgot during this time of "being the best and getting the best" was that God is way smarter than I can ever become. No amount of Internet research, book knowledge, Brad's dental schooling, or support groups would allow me to bypass His knowledge and power. Unfortunately, that realization would take years to hit. My mission during this storm was "survive and advance." Survive the crisis. Advance with knowledge. Survive the storm. Advance toward victory. Whatever it took.

I find it difficult to look at pictures of my life from before Kate's birth. That person—my younger self— was hopeful and innocent. I believed in my own ability to derive success by making good decisions, and only knew positive life circumstances. Now I felt confused, isolated, and abandoned. I didn't know how to navigate these storms.

There was Another who was abandoned too. He wasn't confused though. He was on a mission to save the human race, including me. Though I didn't understand, these hurricanes were teaching me to take part in the sufferings of Christ.

> Survive the crisis. Advance with knowledge. Survive the storm. Advance toward victory. Whatever it took.

# CHAPTER 3

## It's Not About Me

Later on in my second pregnancy, my mom encouraged Brad and me to enjoy a much needed weekend getaway. I was quick to accept her invitation to watch our daughter. My old "entertainer" tendencies were craving travel, adventure, and fun, despite the continued nausea. I was an extrovert who was tired of attending playgroups where I was forced to constantly console my child, unable to interact with the other mothers. I was exhausted from carrying the guilt I felt about my waning confidence that I was a good mom. We felt incredibly guilty leaving Kate with my mom. She was difficult in every sense of the word, but my mom insisted that we get a break.

Brad planned an incredible trip to Boston with multiple surprises for my thirtieth birthday, and we happily escaped with my sister and brother-in-law to meet up with friends. As a child who cherished family unity, I couldn't wait to get away.

That first day in "Bean Town," we explored the downtown area near our hotel, waiting for our reservation at a premier restaurant for dinner. My brother-in-law knew the head chef at this fancy restaurant, and we were guaranteed the best table as we savored the chef's finest dishes. We had also planned to attend a Broadway show with my high school best friend later that night.

Walking down one particular street that afternoon in Boston, I tripped and fell into a pothole. Once we all realized I was fine and had no injuries—nary a pain—we laughed. *Clumsy pregnant woman falls into a pothole!*

Early evening came. Brad and I were in the hotel room getting ready for dinner, and I started hemorrhaging. Rather than calling 9-1-1, Brad called the front desk and they recommended we hail a taxi. The rush hour traffic in downtown Boston would prevent the first responders from responding as quickly as needed.

"A cab will be faster," they told us.

Donned with towels, we took a taxi to Mass General, the hospital with arguably the best neonatal unit in the country.

Looking back, I believe God was developing my dependence on Him during this crisis. I craved entertainment. If He wanted me to bow my knee and submit to His purposes for me, He needed to take away the idol of adventure I had created for myself. This was not a scheme of God's, filled with anger, retribution, or penalty. This was no punishment. It was a loving message wrapped in a carefully planned sequence of events; ones that would eventually help me see His purposes for me. God made me an "entertainer" and an "adventurer," and he fully intended me to live a life full of excitement. However, He intended me to live for His glory and "I" needed to be taken off the throne. My adventurous spirit at that time was about me. He intended to use my spirit for a much greater beauty than I could see.

When we arrived at the hospital, the medical team's assessment was that my placenta was detaching. These are the words spoken by a half-dozen people, ones I remember amidst all the pandemonium in the Emergency Room:

"You're not leaving this hospital."

"You're on strict bed rest."

"Call your mom, because she'll have to move here to help care for your three-year-old."

"Brad can go back to work while your mom lives in Boston with your daughter."

"Since your child has only twenty-three weeks of development, she has a forty percent chance of surviving."

"If she survives, she could potentially have multiple physical and mental challenges."

"We'll have to deliver her early."

That first night, the only questions my shocked brain could ask were, "Really? Another child with medical hardship? Why can't I just enjoy one break? Don't I deserve that?"

Subconsciously, my emotions swirled with this new storm, but all I felt was numbness. Was this another full-blown hurricane? That night, I stared out at Boston Harbor, with all its city lights, as tears streamed down my face. My weekend full of fun and adventure had derailed just like my life. Why me? Why can't I be down in the bustling city having fun like the thousands of others?

Brad returned to the hotel to get some sleep after the initial trauma was over, knowing I was secure in my hospital room. I was overwhelmed . . . and safe for the time being, on strict bed rest.

"Press this button if you have to go to the bathroom," the nurse directed. "Here's the remote control. There are fifty channels. Watch whatever you want, but do *not* get up."

I turned on the TV.

There were two working channels. Not fifty. Forty-eight channels broadcasted static, and one Spanish language channel was available, but I didn't speak or understand Spanish. That left the final option—a stream of infomercials.

I pressed the button the nurse had left for me. No one came. I pressed it fifty times—matching the number of channels I was supposed to have access to as my frustration over losing my weekend getaway succumbed to the panic I felt for my unborn baby. Still no nurse came.

"I could be dead by now," I lamented.

What happened next was a miracle—an inexplicable moment where God stepped down from heaven and pushed play on the TV. When He did, the next thirty-minute infomercial began to air.

"I don't know where you are right now. I don't know if you're lying in a hospital bed or hiding in your closet . . . "

Immediately, I knew I was with God and He was speaking directly to me. "Okay. God. What do you want to tell me?"

I surrendered to God so easily in that hospital bed because for the first time, my eyes were opened to the *possibility* I couldn't handle much more on my own. Weariness is quite an influencing factor as we navigate our life's hurricanes. Lying in that hospital bed with the fresh news of our baby's prognosis hanging over me, I was more open to hearing what God wanted to say, more so than when I relentlessly praised Him.

The infomercial highlighted Max Lucado's newest book at the time called *It's Not About Me*. I became engrossed with the infomercial, which outlined the concept, "It's not about us, it's about God's glory." In His cunning and wildly loving way, God had rendered me unable to move, fixed my eyes on Him, and while He had my attention, gave me a preview of my purpose and life to come.

The moment the infomercial ended, the nurse popped her head into my room.

"What's wrong?"

"You said there are fifty stations. I only have two."

"No," she countered. "There are fifty." She took the remote and changed the channel over and over again. All fifty stations worked perfectly. *Only God.*

I could only offer her a smile. The rest of the weekend, as I was laid up in that hospital room, I sat in a holy confidence that God had a plan, and I just had to ride it out until I understood what else I was supposed to do.

Over the next day or two, the doctors determined my placenta was still intact, but the state of my pregnancy was still in question since they were unsure of the origin of the bleeding. Legally, they couldn't allow me to board a commercial airline in my condition. The doctor said the only way I could get home was if I knew someone with a private plane. Thankfully, we had a family friend who was able to provide one. I was taken directly to the hospital in Charlotte, North Carolina and then discharged to home for modified bed rest.

Once home, I ordered *It's Not About Me* by Max Lucado, but I must not have been ready for the full message yet. When it arrived in the mail, I put it on my nightstand. Even though the concept had impacted me, I wouldn't read it for years.

God put me in that hospital bed first to help me understand the life of never-ending fun and prosperity I longed for was not in His plan. Though, admittedly, adventure is still part of our picture—just not in the way I ever imagined. And second, God gave me a portion of what He would continue to show me over the next decade. He knows we can't take in the magnitude of our stories and the weight of our purposes all at once. God loves us enough to know we can only handle one little piece at a time.

*It's not about you, Tiffany.*

# CHAPTER 4

## Survive and Advance

Once our second daughter was born, I had moments when I blamed God for the new life He had handed us. It certainly felt like Brad and I were given bitter cup after bitter cup to drink. Church and the traditional Christian way of thinking, particularly in our country of plenty, had implied that if we prayed enough or gave enough, we would be blessed. On occasion, we didn't feel or see any of the blessings in our lives. In-between these days filled with the burden of doubt, we tried to trust Him. But our trust was built on the premise that we would be rewarded for being good. My roller coaster ride of faith became emotionally and spiritually taxing.

As with Kate, our new baby was far from easy. She wouldn't sleep. She wouldn't sit in a car seat without screaming. She would scream so much that she vomited. She wouldn't eat. She was colicky, too. I was forced to carry her around in a baby sling or carrier, keeping her moving at all times because her stomach hurt, despite eliminating dairy and everything else that might cause colic.

On top of that, Kate struggled with the change of adding another child to our family. She started acting as if she might be on the autism spectrum, no longer able to sleep by herself—something we had finally achieved not long before the birth of our second child. Ordinary noises bothered her. Things like the hum of the refrigerator or a plane's engine overhead. All things related to her senses were amplified. Noises terrified her to the point of barely being able to leave the house.

The separation anxiety we had always struggled with intensified and she screamed tirelessly. The nurse who handed her to us so many years ago had been correct. She did house quite the pair of lungs in that tiny body of hers. On the other side of the coin, noises disrupted her in every way possible. She was even kicked out of preschool because of her relentless crying. (One fine individual had the audacity to send me an article explaining how kids who are kicked out of preschool have an eighty-five percent chance of ending up in prison later in life.) This catapulted the overwhelming thought—the lie—I had been wrestling with over the years into the stratosphere.

"You're a failure."

An area of pride, which I wasn't able to understand or articulate at the time, was that I expected my children to have the same intelligence level as me. I certainly didn't see this as pride, however. It was setting an expectation that God would later deal with in a beautiful way. Why do we think we can define, as a society, what intelligence is? Only God can define intelligence, a beautiful intelligence that defies society's boundaries. Kate defies these boundaries because she is His creation.

After an initial diagnosis of sensory integration disorder and initiating therapy that never helped, we learned Kate has borderline intelligence. Even though I knew it wasn't any fault of mine, that label gutted me. As a high-achieving and successful rule-follower, I struggled with parenting a child who wasn't cooperating, coloring outside society's behavioral expectations, crying uncontrollably, and not grasping preschool-level concepts. When the preschool was not able to handle her, I was devastated. Every minute of life felt serious. The final remnants of "fun" Tiffany slipped away under the growing storm waves of depression.

I couldn't shake the hopelessness, and God became my punching bag. I blamed Him for our family's struggles. I made Him liable for giving me more than I could handle.

Kate was not "typical," and at this point, while still parenting another difficult newborn, I realized our oldest would need to learn how to manage a life-time full of difficulties. But I was still determined to heal her myself. After all, the solution wasn't coming from God, so I decided to step in and try to direct our own outcomes. "If God won't, I will."

I assumed there must be a solution somewhere—one I had to find. He wasn't leading us to answers or resolving the chaos. So, I continued my mission to survive and advance. Looking back, I realize this was a symptom of the desperation I felt. I kept thinking, "Having children is way harder than it was ever supposed to be."

It didn't take long for me to jump to the next assumption and lie: God didn't love me. At the minimum, I believed He had left me—abandoned me. With that mindset, I lost all joy during this season of parenting.

On the exterior, no one knew the emotional and spiritual trauma I was experiencing. I hoarded these negative thoughts and emotions and kept everything to myself, not wanting to admit defeat or failure. I only confided in Brad. At church, I put on a happy mask, and my worship looked genuine to everyone around me. On the inside, anger started to boil.

Remembering this hurricane, which had now strengthened to a Category 3, I always picture Darth Vader. Over time, he transformed into more of a machine than a man. That was what was happening to my heart. More jaded. Darker. Secretly tilting toward hostility. While I never completely lost faith in God, I was determined to beat the storm back with my own perseverance, intellect, and resourcefulness. I fought the hurricane of parenting medically and emotionally challenging children with everything I could. Shock and denial, the cornerstones of grief, lay in the weeds, and I couldn't accept the idea that there was nothing I could do—that this was the life God had handed me as punishment for a reason I couldn't decipher. So, I marched on.

As we all know, hurricanes are forces to be reckoned with, and they don't bow down to someone's will and just scoot away. In reality, denial of the ferocity of the storm is what gets people killed.

When Kate was six years old, we decided to start looking for schools for her. We had her evaluated by the local public school, but at the time felt her anxiety required a smaller institution, a Christian environment. We discovered her academics and IQ were below the acceptable standard for *every* private Christian institution in our area.

Each school I called sounded excited until I presented them with her testing results. Then, they all gave me the same response. "We feel that your child would be more successful somewhere else. Since we are a college preparatory institution, we just don't feel like she would be a good fit."

I felt defeated and frustrated when they kept talking about college. I wasn't trying to get my six-year-old into college! I was trying to get her into kindergarten. Again, just like in high school, I was also wondering why "Christian" institutions were only taking kids who fit in the "box." Wouldn't Jesus take the "least of these?" I understand it takes money and resources. Not all schools have those resources. I understand the complexity of special needs. I do. But why isn't this a priority among Jesus followers? I still have these questions today.

Finally, I called Huntersville Christian Academy. It was the last school I was willing to call. If this school didn't take her then I would end my search. I sat in the headmaster's office waiting to hear the same response when she looked at me and said, "Listen, I looked over Kate's testing. According to the academic rigor here, she may struggle. However, last night our Board and I prayed. We believe the Lord wants us to accept your daughter as she is."

I tear up thinking about this even now. This school later became Lake Norman Christian. To this day, all three of my children have been loved by this school. Their teachers have loved my children. Their teachers have been Jesus to our family. I am still thankful for that sweet headmaster who looked to Jesus, not society, for direction about accepting my child. The academic rigor was eventually too difficult for Kate. But for six years, she was loved as she was. Loved without society's boundaries.

\*\*\*

Back when I was in high school, my track coach had asked me to run a 10K (6.2 miles) on a Sunday, just for fun. He promised me it would be a relaxing and easy race.

Things changed at the starting line. My coach mentioned that a competitor, whom I was going to race in Regionals a few days later, was running the 10k too. My ultra-competitive juices were primed and started flowing through my veins. I *had* to beat her. I knew racing was eighty percent mental. "If I want to beat her at Regionals, I must beat her today."

It seemed I had been born ready for challenges and being the youngest child, I felt I had to prove I could do anything at all times. Running and winning races were part of "anything."

My coach warned me, "You shouldn't race her. Take it easy, your regional meet is next week."

His statement, meant to take some of the pressure off, in reality, spurred me on even more. My nagging hip problem from middle school had become fairly problematic at this point, but I wouldn't stop running. I didn't care.

When the gun went off, I ran each of the six and two-tenths miles faster than I should have. I didn't pace myself for the long haul. By mile four, I was dry-heaving, but I refused to stop. Spectators and coaches were yelling at me to bail out as I passed them. I ignored their shouts and kept going.

I ended up beating her, but I also threw my hip out in the final strides. It was so bad that I was not able to run in the regional meet a few days later. That has always been my mentality—ignore the pain. *No pain, no gain.*

"Beat yesterday. Beat everyone's expectations. Work hard. You will be rewarded." I think my hip was always something God was going to allow to break. My hip represented my will and my control. God wanted something different from me and for me. Unfortunately, I wasn't ready to give it all up just yet.

*\*\*\**

My hip healed in high school, and even though a chiropractor encouraged me never to run again, I continued running off and on throughout my young adult life. My mileage increased significantly after the birth of our second child. As part of my

> That has always been my mentality—ignore the pain. No pain, no gain.

"survive and advance" mentality, running became an outlet for the anger, disappointment, and rejection I felt believing God had abandoned me. It was becoming more difficult to fake happiness.

Three miles turned into four, which turned into five, and so on. *Beat yesterday.* My teenage mantra had never subsided. With the lone-ranger, "survive and advance" mission I created and accepted, I had built up an impressive tolerance for pain. Physical pain. Emotional pain. You name it pain. I simply motored on through, fighting for whatever finish line I had placed in front of myself. During this storm, the finish line meant raising healthy, happy children and a return to the fun life I missed. Life was definitely about me.

When not running, I researched. Hours and hours would go by while I sought out answers to the problems my children were experiencing.

*Sensory processing disorder*
*Incessant screaming*
*Separation anxiety*
*Chronic illnesses*
*Moodiness*
*Difficulty with school*
*Insomnia*

Both girls couldn't sleep by themselves, so we put them in a room together with an extra mattress for Brad to lay with them for hours until they were asleep. Kate would lay awake, making sure Brad didn't close his eyes. It was torture. We were exhausted day and night. All around me, mothers were reading and sharing parenting books about letting kids "cry it out," which was a popular philosophy at the time.

"You just need to let them cry it out," everyone told me.

Every time we tried it, my children worsened. We tried, trust me we tried. But every time we did, we ended up cleaning up vomit.

"I really am the worst mother ever," I thought. Mother's guilt slithered into condemnation. The enemy was having a play date of his own inside my soul.

At one point, I even blamed Brad and his genetic coding for our kids' struggles. Thankfully, our marriage woes had begun to subside. Brad is an easy person to be married to, and I think he figured out how to relate to me in the midst of our parenting trials.

"Mommy. Mommy! I just swallowed all those rocks that were over there."

Weird symptoms, such as exaggerations and paranoia, even hallucinations, filled our days. Our daughters weren't making friends. Our second daughter wasn't struggling with preschool concepts and academics like Kate had—

she is quite intelligent—but she struggled with shyness, separation anxiety, and a fear of throwing up.

As a former social butterfly, these relational and emotional struggles clobbered the core of how I had envisioned my children would be—really, should be. My dreams of not only having healthy and happy but socially mature kids dissolved into the floodwaters this hurricane continued to provoke.

I suffered in complete silence though. This was only my fault. I wanted people to think I had it together. I didn't want people to know I was a failure. I tried to fit in with friends and neighbors.

Only Brad (and my family) knew the complete truth of our home life. My family, particularly my mom and sister, were (and still are) a huge support system. My sister has been a lifeline for our family. She has sacrificed many nights to take our children so that we can get a break. She often gets emotional, even now, watching our situation. I am so grateful for her support.

However, no one could truly understand the force of our storm without living under our roof. At some point, the happy mask started to slide off my face. The nightmare of our home life finally stripped me of the energy required to continue being fake. I couldn't pretend to be fine for one more minute. My close neighbors and good friends could read between the lines, and their support was something I badly needed. Looking back, I know they wanted to help earlier than I probably realized. It was time for me to be "real." What so many don't understand is that your "real" friends are waiting for you to be honest so they can help.

I stayed home and questioned God as I navigated the tornadoes that would spin up out of the hurricane on a daily basis. My parents looked at us and our lives and encouraged us not to have more children.

"You have enough already," they said. No one knew we were already pregnant.

When the test indicated our third child was on the way, I immediately drove to Brad's dental office and blamed him as if it was his fault! That night we were filled with panic.

"Lord, I don't know if we can handle another child."

To that, God said to my spirit, "I know you can't handle another child, but I never said I wouldn't give you only what you can handle. I will always give you more so you will finally trust me to handle all your crises." I didn't hear that message right away. It would be years later—years full of more storms—before this truth would set in and I would accept it and understand it as *grace*.

# CHAPTER 5

## The Deluge

During my third pregnancy, my hyperemesis gravidarum was the worst it had ever been. I lost thirty pounds, becoming emaciated. The doctors put me on four different medications to keep me out of the hospital. I ate one plain waffle per day, and if I moved, I threw up. No one could cook in the house because any smell would trigger me. There was no TV, no phone calls, no bright lights. Depression is almost the only emotion one can feel when experiencing this type of nausea. It was like having a stomach virus all day every day for four months. Again, I couldn't even cry. If I did, I threw up. I could only think and allow one tear to slide down my cheeks. Lying still in bed 24/7, my mom took over parenting our two girls during the day while Brad was at work. I have very few memories of our daughters for about a four-month period.

"What is happening?" This question haunted my thoughts.

Kate had already been to dozens of specialists with no clear answers. No one could figure out her diagnosis. By age seven, we started various medications, including antipsychotics and SSRIs. Nothing worked. When she picked up an illness, like a cold or flu, every other weird symptom was magnified. She still wasn't learning appropriately, she was developmentally delayed, but she wasn't labeled with any "known" diagnosis, such as autism.

We hired a full-time shadow to accompany Kate during kindergarten, a woman who was truly an angel to us at the time and still is today. She left her teaching job to help us. However, despite her incredible call to support a weary family, it was still difficult for me to relax. I was constantly waiting for the phone calls and anticipating the anxiety of Kate's inability to complete kindergarten-level tasks and repeated crying and OCD behaviors. At the same time, our second child entered preschool, and she struggled with separation anxiety more than anything else.

Then our son was born on a beautiful October day in 2008. He was a big baby and the C-section went as planned. The first year with him was decent compared to the other two. He ate well, slept well, and seemed to be an easier baby. He still struggled with colic and acid reflux but was more typical in terms of what many parents endure with newborns.

However, shortly after he turned one in 2009, the H1N1 pandemic was raging. He was diagnosed with this horrible strain of flu the same day I was. I felt like death and understood for the first time why people can die from the flu. Panic had been ensuing throughout the country.

Seemingly overnight, he experienced the most severe onset of these same weird symptoms his sisters had, but they were worse. He had been sleeping in his room, eating well, and was healthy. The next day, it seemed he had truly lost his mind. He started walking in repeated circles and hallucinating. He would look at the baby camera in his room with wide eyes, pointing and indicating to us that he could see Thomas the Train in his bedroom. He woke up eight to ten times each night. His eating became very restrictive (something that would continue for the next seven years). I thought maybe he was experiencing a reaction to the Tamiflu, which the doctor had prescribed for the H1N1 virus. Then, he started expressing bizarre repetitive behaviors. So, I took him to a neurologist.

"He seems perfectly neurotypical for his age. He's just anxious." What? Just anxious? This wasn't just anxiety. He was walking in circles for hours, crying, hitting, and clawing at us if we disciplined him in any way. It was like he had the terrible twos at age one. But it was the terrible twos on steroids.

I begged them to keep looking.

"You don't understand! Two weeks ago, he was a chill, happy, healthy, normal kid. Now, he's acting crazy." The flu had also spread to our middle child, and her symptoms—fear of swallowing things, fear of throwing up, and separation anxiety—intensified as well.

Our son worsened with each passing year. *Yes, years.* He wasn't improving with time. His peculiar directives toward family members grew scary, forcing us to watch certain things, say certain things, and threatening to scream, become vindictive, or rage if we didn't comply. I gave in to his demands because I didn't know what else to do. I was just trying to survive.

"Fine. You want to watch this video on a loop? Go ahead."

"At least he is contained," I thought to myself. This perpetuated the last few years of self-deprecation, which I had been battling. "You are the worst mother ever," I convinced myself.

If we didn't say the words he wanted to hear, he'd repeatedly tell us to "Say you're sorry. Say you're sorry. Say you're sorry," until we apologized and said the "right" thing at least twenty or thirty times. By age four, we had taken our son to multiple specialists, hoping for an answer to this wild behavior. He had obvious OCD, but the DSM

(Diagnostic Manual) doesn't allow for an official diagnosis until age five. They threw more diagnoses our way.

*Generalized anxiety*
*Selective mutism*
*Language processing disorder*

In hindsight, his sudden change in personality and behavior was a textbook case for one particular diagnosis, but no one yet knew the driving force behind all of our children's struggles. It is important to note that the very professionals we were taking our kids to weren't well-informed about this combination of symptoms, and this should be concerning to all providers.

We now had three kids with anxiety and weird manifestations for unknown reasons. Our two youngest fought going to school. While they wouldn't admit it openly, their separation anxiety was overwhelming. I was never able to watch any of my children bound off to school, smiling and waving to me from the classroom door after carpool drop off. Unlike most other mothers, volunteering or attending school events was incredibly difficult and added additional anxiety instead of joy.

Unlike most other mothers, volunteering or attending school events was incredibly difficult and added additional anxiety instead of joy.

My kids couldn't cope with me leaving afterward, crying and holding onto my legs, begging me to take them with me. These situations stole my joy. I constantly worried what behavior would manifest, so I strategically picked activities that were at the end of the day so I could take them with me.

Two kids were now in speech therapy. Two kids were in occupational therapy. One child had a full-time tutor. Brad and I were spending thousands of dollars and getting nowhere fast. Despite all this, I refused to say my children had any special needs. That was a term of finality. I was not willing to admit our current situation might never improve.

Our marriage was continually impacted. Brad was forced to sleep with our son. I slept in Kate's room. I believed without a doubt that God had abandoned me. I still hadn't shared our struggles with many people outside our home. I knew we would be judged. I knew what people would say:

*You need to discipline him.*
*Don't give into his demands.*
*You shouldn't sleep in your kids' rooms.*

I also refrained from telling our pediatrician because I assumed the judgment would come from there, too. I imagined the doctor saying, "You've got a behavior problem you need to nip in the bud."

Failure. Failure. Failure.

Meanwhile, when I was able to leave the kids with Brad, I ran more and more. The miles piled up—five to eight miles nearly every day. In essence, I ran because for the first time in my life, I felt I had no control over the circumstances or the direction my life had taken. My fitness level and the number on the scale morphed into what some may call addictions. I *had* to weigh a certain amount, and I *had* to run a certain distance. My own OCD tendencies emerged as I grasped for control of something. My house became spotless as I feverishly cleaned every corner, top to bottom. I searched for any ounce of happiness I might find in being able to control something—anything.

I felt beaten down. Years upon years of medical and behavioral chaos and mystery. The swirling hurricanes continued to make landfall all over my life, bending my soul in ways I felt sure would cause me to break. Something had to give.

# CHAPTER 6

## Fight For Your Marriage

O n our wedding days, we recite our vows and repeat the line "in sickness and in health." Those of us with atypical children, or children with various health crises, would like to turn this one line into an essay. After all, most couples are only thinking about themselves when they make this promise. They aren't thinking of the possibility of atypical children. One line wasn't enough to capture what our future entailed. We should have said:

*In the case your child may be diagnosed with a life-altering illness, condition, or any long list of diseases that incapacitate your child's neuro-*

typical reasoning faculties, you may be tempted to lose your mind. The term "in sickness" may or may not include blaming each other incessantly for their genetics, especially the uncle with "issues" that may or may not be the source of chromosomal mishap. You may also blame a spouse, name not mentioned, for his or her job that seems more important than your child's health, the anger issues that will arise because, and again, we won't mention names, one spouse is doing ALL the research, going to ALL the doctor appointments and assisting in ALL the therapies. This anger may or may not arise occasionally, but daily, due to the insanity constantly flooding your household.

In addition, "sickness" may also include, but is not limited to, spending way more money than you can possibly produce. Insurance may or may NOT cover most of your expenses, which will cause additional stress and calamity in the household. Your child's future doctors may or may NOT understand your child's diagnosis, which may or may not cause you to become a psychiatrist, immunologist, neurologist, nutritionist, and educational specialist via Internet training.

Last, but certainly not least, the term "sickness" may or may not cause at least one of you, and we certainly won't name this name, to lose any sem-

*blance of the "health" you once had due to eating more chocolate, junk (or even health) food, and drinks than one should consume. This "sickness" may thereby cause an increase in weight, blood pressure, sleepless nights, and a future diagnosis of anxiety disorders. You may or may not eventually get to a point where you just DON'T CARE.*

*So, enjoy your beautiful day. Enjoy the blue skies. You're married!!! Remember these vows are just possible **unlikely** outcomes. Good luck!*

In all seriousness, I wrote this from the heart. I know many of you would have written similar vows. Looking back on the many hurricanes we have faced over the years, I want to reflect on what I believe to be the reason our marriage not only survived, but thrived.

The attention that is required of parents of children with health crises is overwhelming. That attention can affect the marriage negatively in a number of ways. Brad and I were certainly not immune to any of it.

We were fortunate enough to have received marriage counseling with the *2 Becoming One* material my parents wrote. We learned biblical principles that provided a blueprint of how to survive a marriage full of trials.

1. **The first principle was that together, male and female, we reflect God in completion.**

    Genesis 1:27 says, "Then God said, "Let us make man in Our image, according to Our likeness; God created man in His own image, in the image of God He created him; male and female He created them."

God is one hundred percent both male and female. Together, we reflect His image, His glory. We were not to become like each other but reflect the totality of male and female joined together to support, uplift, and complement the other. *Two* had to become *one*.

2. **The second principle is from Genesis 2, which states that we are God's gift to one another, each with a set of strengths and weaknesses.**

Genesis 2:18 says, "Then the Lord God said, "It is not good for the man to be alone; I will make a helper suitable for him."

So when we encounter trials of any sort, we are to look at each other, knowing God provided for one with the other, so that together we will weather any storm that comes our way. We are God's provision for each other, with all our strengths *and* weaknesses. We are to complete each other, not fight against each other.

3. **The third principle we learned is that trials are a natural part of life, and we are not to blame the other for what we are going through.**

James 1: 2–4 says, "Consider it all joy, my brethren, when you encounter various trials, knowing that the testing of your faith produces endurance. And let endurance have its perfect result, so that you may be made perfect and complete, lacking in nothing."

Often, we (married couples) do blame each other. We compartmentalize our suffering instead of doing it together and point fingers as if the other is the cause of our trials.

*You never help me.*
*You don't care.*
*You are so insensitive.*

We are not supposed to be surprised when we encounter trials, although I venture to say we are *always* surprised. We were surprised when I experienced hyperemesis gravidarum in each pregnancy. We were surprised when Kate was sick all the time, and we had no answers to her condition, mentally or physically. We were surprised when all three of our kids developed debilitating symptoms of a mysterious origin. We

were surprised, but because of these principles, we were able to see that our problems
weren't each other.

4.  **The last principle I want to share will explain
    why most of us don't see eye to eye with our
    spouse. It will explain why we often feel alone
    and unsupported as opposed to supported
    and together.**

    Genesis 3:16 (To the Woman)

    "I will greatly multiply
    Your pain in childbirth,
    In pain you will bring forth children;
    Yet your desire will be for your husband."

    Genesis 3:17–19 (To the Man)

    "Cursed is the ground because of you;
    In toil you will eat of it
    All the days of your life.
    Both thorns and thistles it shall grow
    for you;
    And you will eat the plants of the field;
    By the sweat of your face
    You will eat bread,
    Till you return to the ground,
    Because from it you were taken;|
    For you are dust,
    And to dust you shall return."

For most of the families who have atypical children, oftentimes the wife feels like she is doing all the research, attending all the doctor appointments, meeting with all the teachers, and planning the educational support. She may feel like her husband isn't interested in helping her with those activities. Sometimes, her husband may struggle with believing the diagnosis, which causes even more strife.

Brad and I struggled with all these things. I, too, felt like I did most of the research and appointments. I felt like his leaving the craziness of our household and "escaping" to work was a gift.

In our marriage, Brad was constantly burdened with his dental practice. When owning a business, there is inevitable pressure—managing people, patients, and finances. He was (and is) under insurmountable stress as he provides for all the expenses flying out of our bank account. Neither of us communicated properly, and our struggles and assumptions smoldered under the surface. Fortunately, Brad, because of our marriage counseling background, recognized this issue and began to actively participate in the research and decision-making.

Genesis 3 explains why we, as married couples, struggle so much with this balance. Wives, the Bible explains, "In pain you will bring forth children." This does not only refer to childbirth; that was covered in the prior line. It means that we will have pain for our children forever! This resonates so deeply for me. When our children are in pain, we are in pain. When they suffer, we suffer. When they have a bad day, we have a bad day. For mothers, whether you are a homemaker or work outside the home, for better or for worse, we tend to evaluate our success as a mom based on our child's happiness and contentment.

Now look at how the man's work was affected. "In toil you will eat of it, All the days of your life. Both thorns and thistles it shall grow for you." Men are constantly toiling over their need to be useful, productive, and needed. They want to provide for the family and a failure to do so causes deep-rooted insecurity. They wake up needing to feel useful and respected. Their measure of success is how well they are providing for the needs of their family.

Genesis 1, 2, and 3 give us a clear picture of God's plan for marriage. He tells us what went wrong with our first parents, and the issues continue to this day. By understanding these principles, when the winds blow and the storms rage, our house will stand on a firm foundation.

> Genesis 1, 2, and 3 give us a clear picture of God's plan for marriage.

Parenting children with any type of issue can be challenging, but doing it alone is that much harder. We need to remember that we are not wrestling against each other, we are wrestling hurricanes. Neither your spouse, nor you are the enemy. As Ephesians 6:12 teaches and I paraphrase, "For our struggle is not against flesh and blood (spouse) but against Satan, who wants you to think it's your spouse." We must fight for our marriages.

*For more information on *2 Becoming One* and Christian Family Life, please visit www.christianfamilylife.com.

# Interlude

I believe all circumstances are engineered by God. I love when events and people collide in a meaningful way. A *kairos* moment is experienced as God enters our space and things change, we're changed. *Kairos* is from Ancient Greek, meaning an opportune moment, one ripe for action or decision. God loves us so much that I believe He designed us to appreciate, even treasure, these *kairos* moments.

God knew I was looking for—and needed—a dramatic *kairos* moment when I was lying in that hospital bed in Boston, staring at infomercials on the only available TV station during my second pregnancy. He knew I would respond. He also knew it wouldn't be for some time. Things would have to get a lot worse before I would be ready to grasp the full measure of His message to me: *It's not about you.*

God also knew that at this point in my life I needed another *kairos* moment. I had moved into a dark place. A fork in the road. Darth Vader's machine was taking over. I was angry and frustrated with a God who promised He would be there for me. Instead, I felt abandoned.

I had a recurring dream where I was searching in the darkness for light. I would click light switch after light switch to no avail. Darkness. Why couldn't I feel Him? Why wouldn't He answer me? Why wouldn't He heal my children? I had longed to experience the life I thought everyone else was experiencing. I thought their lives were easier, brighter, and more joyful. I was enveloped in a world all about *me*. I couldn't see others accurately because my circumstances blinded me. I no longer prayed. I no longer sought Him. Every time I did, there was no answer. Or at least not the answer I was looking for.

Not too long ago, I had another dream just like the ones I used to have. I was in a room full of darkness. I opened two double doors searching for light—for Jesus. As I opened the doors another set of doors appeared. Then another, then another, and another. As the doors opened, my fervor to find and grasp the light became insatiable. I frantically began to open the doors faster and faster. Finally, the final doors opened and . . . darkness. I was perplexed, and then right as I woke up, I felt Him standing right next to me. Jesus had been right next to me the whole time. What I didn't understand was that He was there the whole time, standing right next to me *in* the darkness.

One morning in the spring of 2011, while my kids were at school and preschool, I sat and stared outside at the beautiful day—the blue sky, blooming flowers, and lush lawns. The scenery was bright, but my heart was dark. I hadn't prayed or talked to God in months. I knew it was a "fork in the road" moment. I knew the path I was on was leading me into a darkness that wouldn't lead to peace.

So, like a spoiled seven-year-old, I told God, "I'm not praying today. I'm not ready to talk to you. But I will read your Word." I yelled in my head, "God, I'm mad at you! I didn't ask for this suffering!"

Almost immediately, I heard a small, still voice say to my heart, "Yes you did." What?

"No I didn't!" I exclaimed.

Then, the *kairos* moment. I remembered that day in college when I asked God to teach me, *at all costs*, how to glorify Him. The memory silenced me. Had I asked for this? Was this suffering part of His plan? His good plan? Was it good? How could it be?

> What I didn't understand was that He was there the whole time, standing right next to me in the darkness.

I wasn't sure what the answer was but I was interested to find out. That day, I read one verse. The next day I read two verses. The verses turned into chapters and before I knew it, I was reading the entire Bible.

Day in and day out, I read the Bible as if it was the first time I had seen it. I was amazed at the dysfunction of the characters and innately knew, for the first time, that I was one of them! I started calling my mom who had studied and taught the Bible all her life. I had experienced an epiphany of sorts.

"Mom the Bible is full of dysfunctional people, and I'm one of them!"

The internal realization hit me hard. All of the sudden, I was David who had ordered a man murdered. I was a murderer. I was a prostitute. I was unfaithful. I was capable of every sin ever committed! In sliding doors, I am every Adam and every Eve. I am a sinner who needs the Cross. **I am a . . . wretch**. At age thirty-six, I realized in the next beat of my heart that I was every bit the wretch from "Amazing Grace." Yet there was no shame in these revelations. It was a joyous moment. I realized why Jesus had to die for me. Thirty years earlier, I had invited Jesus into my heart, but on this day, it was the first day I felt redeemed.

This redeemed wretch would never be the same. I now understood why I felt better in high school when I was with the partiers—the "sinners" if you will. I was one of them. I finally understood why the perfection of "religion" didn't provide comfort for me. Jesus wasn't religious.

I knew why my college friends comforted me. They loved, just like Jesus. Jesus went to parties and hung out with the sinners and those who were diseased and warty and wretched. He hung out with me, right next to me, *in* the darkness. On that sunny, spring day, I understood He had a plan for me. I felt freedom.

But does realizing that God is standing next to you in the darkness mean you are immune to further suffering? No. And I was about to be tested yet again . . .

> I finally understood why the perfection of "religion" didn't provide comfort for me. Jesus wasn't religious.

# PART II

*"All through Scripture, what God is trying
to bring us back to is this: '. . . if you
see me, and your passion becomes
My honor and My glory, then I am free
to go to work in you and through you.'"*
—John Maisel

# CHAPTER 7

## The "-ectomy" of Me

I n the summer of 2011, we hired a medical team consisting of a neuropsychologist, social worker, and various doctors to assess Kate, who was still struggling with learning and medical illnesses. We spent thousands of dollars, and in the end, we sat before a panel of experts.

I'll never forget what the lead doctor said to us. "Your child just doesn't fit into any perfectly square box. I know you've spent a lot of money on these evaluations, but we can't give her any diagnosis. It's not trauma. It's not Asperger's (the unofficial term for high-functioning autism). Her IQ assessments show the craziest results we've ever seen. In my twenty-five years of work, I've never seen anyone like her."

On the drive home, we sat in silence, trying to process what we just heard. *She doesn't fit into any perfectly square box.* For the first time, I succumbed to the truth I had been avoiding and unwilling to accept for ten long years.

"No one is going to be able to tell us if she will be OK. No one is going to be able to tell us about her or our future." I realized there is only One who knows our futures, and all this was in His hands.

I was, for the first time, at peace. From that day forward, I knew that I could never expect a doctor to tell me Kate's prognosis or promise a secure future for her. They didn't know. I wanted someone to tell me that she was going to be fine. They couldn't. I think many of us look to doctors. But only God knows the future.

In that moment, I caught a glimpse of what it feels like to be in the eye of a hurricane. The sun was shining through the swirling winds, still spinning all around me. It felt warm and peaceful. Looking straight up, I could see the sun. But the reprieve would only last a moment. Crashing thunder could be heard in the distance.

About that time, in the summer of that same year, I started seeing an oncologist/hematologist for chronic iron deficiency, which I had dealt with for nearly my entire life. They decided to start yearly iron infusions to avoid constant side effects from large doses of oral iron. While I saw this doctor for hematology, he was also an oncologist and treated patients with cancer.

During one iron infusion, I sat in the chair at the medical clinic, among a sea of patients undergoing chemotherapy. Next to me was one of those patients, a woman receiving treatment for breast cancer. I felt guilty as I looked at her. My IV held an iron supplement, not the life-saving poison that hers contained.

I decided to strike up a conversation. Instantly, as if God put the notion smack in the middle of my heart, I knew I was going to relate to her. In the deep parts of my soul, a realization was born, not of fear but of truth.

That evening, I looked at Brad and blurted out, "I think I have breast cancer."

"What? Did you feel something? What do you mean?"

At thirty-six years old and with no family history, it didn't make sense. But I knew. Again, it wasn't an irrational (or even rational) fear. It felt more like reality that hadn't been realized yet. However, I dropped it—it did sound quite absurd, didn't it?—and within twenty-four hours, I didn't think about cancer again.

Two months later, during a regular check-up with my doctor, he informed me he had treated a rash of patients with breast cancer. He advised me to get a mammogram. I still didn't remember the revelation I had experienced during my chat with the woman receiving chemotherapy.

During my mammogram a week later, the technician acted strangely right after she took the image. She later told me that she put my mammogram on the top of the pile so that the doctor would view it first. The next day, Charlotte Radiology called and said they saw a suspicious mass on my images. At that point, I remembered the revelation from a few months earlier. They told me they wanted me to come in the next day.

The following morning, after taking more images, having an ultrasound, and undergoing a biopsy, the doctor informed me that he was relatively certain I had breast cancer. He mentioned that it was most likely caught early, and the ultrasound of my lymph nodes didn't indicate spread of the cancer.

I felt incredibly calm. After all, I had been through deep darkness without answers the past ten years. This was caught early. It was a named entity. There was no mystery. That was a win, right? I had experienced repeated trauma after trauma. I was used to life not turning out rainbows and puffy clouds. I also felt Jesus sitting right next to me in the darkness. I immediately texted Brad at work, something I later regretted. I was the one who seemed to know deep in my soul that this was another part of my journey. He would have to watch me suffer. I should have called but instead I typed:

*They are pretty sure I have breast cancer. But they caught it early.*

Brad was at work and this caused great distress for him. I should have known. I had watched all three of my children suffer over and over. In that moment, it was nice that for once, I was the one suffering. I didn't realize it then, but I felt relief that I would be the one to feel pain this time. Not them. The surgeon who did the biopsy was amazed at my stoic strength. After he had told me I most likely had breast cancer and I didn't shed a single tear, he asked, "What have you been through? No one responds like this."

Over the next hour, I told him about my children. I told him about the pain of watching my children suffer and how this would be part of my story, too. It was a story I knew God was perfectly penning, even in the midst of a possible cancer diagnosis.

On a "Carolina blue," picture-perfect October 3rd, the Charlotte Observer printed much of its newspaper in pink for #breastcancerawarenessday. That very day, the doctor's office called to confirm my diagnosis. Cancer. I kept that newspaper and still have it today.

It was stage zero cancer. The cancer had been detected in the "party stage", as I call it. The party stage is where all the cancer was hanging out, trying to form a mass but hadn't quite succeeded and never invaded surrounding tissue. The doctor said, "This will be a bump on your road. We caught this early. Hopefully you will not need additional treatment besides removing the cancer."

That day, calling my family and closest friends was difficult. Everyone assumed I was going to die. One family member stated, "I guess God didn't think you had enough already." After a few hours and through the grapevine, even friends from high school started contacting me, telling me how much they loved me back when we were teenagers.

I appreciated the sentiments (truly). I had never felt so loved. However, earlier that day, I was convinced it wouldn't be a long road, but their concern concerned me. I was exhausted. My children were still completely dysfunctional. My problems were certainly still raging.

Finally in bed for the night, I asked God for one word. "God, I'm too tired. Just give me one verse." He had spoken to me a few months earlier through Scripture. "What do You want from me?" I opened my Bible, and I had already highlighted I Peter 3:15:

"But in your hearts revere Christ as Lord. Always be prepared to give an answer to everyone who asks you to give the reason for the hope that you have. But do this with gentleness and respect."

God was clear. I was to suffer for His glory. I was to experience pain so that others could gain my knowledge. Fear was replaced with peace. The coming distress, as well as the current suffering I had been enduring for ten years, was for others to see why I have hope.

The following day, I saw Max Lucado's book, *It's Not About Me* on my nightstand, covered in a thin layer of dust. The night following my cancer diagnosis, I read it in its entirety. I guess I was finally ready to hear God's full message for me.

When I finished the book, I resumed my daily calls to my mom.

"Wait! It's not about me! He is using me. This is all for His glory!" God had a plan.

I urged my sisters to get a mammogram as well. After all they had the same genetics as me, and we had absolutely no family history of breast cancer. I was only thirty-six and they were both older than me. They went in for their mammograms the following week, all of us thinking it was simply an overabundance of precaution.

My oldest sister, age forty at the time and who lives in Atlanta, called me after her mammogram. "You are never going to believe this. They immediately saw a concerning mass and they wanted to biopsy."

I quickly said to her "They are just being cautious. What are the chances?" Then, the biopsy came back. Cancer.

My poor mother. In two weeks' time, two of her young daughters were diagnosed with breast cancer. Genetic testing revealed we had a gene called BARD 1. It isn't as serious but does cause an elevated risk in both breast and ovarian cancer. My mother carries the same gene, though it had never manifested. She felt responsible for our diagnoses. It was an emotional time.

The following months consisted of blood tests, scans, research, and more doctors' appointments than either of us could process. Both of us had other areas in both breasts that appeared suspicious. Our surgeons individually recommended for both of us to have double mastectomies. "-ectomy" comes from a Greek word for "removal of." It was apparent that during this time, God was starting to remove "me" from my narrative and replace my self-focus with Him.

It was comforting to go through this with my sister, but painful all at the same time. Once again, I felt almost comforted knowing that for once, I could bear the pain instead of watching my children suffer. But I had to watch my sister suffer. Double mastectomies are emotional. It's a loss that can make you feel less like a woman. I wondered, "How would I feel? How would she feel?" The pain didn't seem daunting to me but to see my sister in pain . . . that was unbearable. I was tired of seeing people I loved in pain.

In addition, my husband who had endured all of what I had, was now going to be the primary caregiver of our anxiety-ridden children while also taking care of me. Brad was (and still is) my hero. He had to help me through twelve major surgeries and countless minor procedures and surgeries. "In sickness and in health" doesn't accurately contain enough words to express what he endured during these years. He took care of our children and me without any complaints. He has been amazing. But he would tell you that we learned together—learned that sometimes all you can do is get up every day, survive, and advance.

Both of our cancers, though stage zero, were relatively aggressive. We couldn't schedule our mastectomies at the same time because my mother had to care for us and help us with our children. My sister also had three children and lived in a different city.

They opted to perform my double mastectomy first on 11/11/11 at 11:00 a.m. Another *kairos* moment. The morning of the surgery, I lay on the gurney. Questions loomed. "What would it be like? Would I be deformed? Would I feel normal ever again?" Brad and my parents stood next to me, holding my hand before the medical staff took

> "In sickness and in health" doesn't accurately contain enough words to express what he endured during these years.

me back. Tears filled all of our eyes. Their little girl was about to be cut and changed forever. It was emotional. I cry every time I think about it. It was an unknown road but one in which I was sure would make me stronger somehow. I posted the following excerpt on Facebook the day before:

> *This morning I ran my last run before the double mastectomy tomorrow. As I ran I couldn't help but think about this course I'm signed up to run starting tomorrow that I know nothing about. Everyone's versions of the course are different and unique – as will be mine.*

> *But, I started learning a long time ago that it's really not all about me. I've learned that most things in life don't fit in a **perfectly square box**. That my strength and my endurance always eventually fail. But, God's strength becomes resilience. God's endurance produces character and God's peace is eternal. I know I'm not the only one looking up at a hill and wondering how high it goes. But, if we only focus on the hill, we will miss the blessing on the other side.*

*Thank you for all of your prayers! I will never be able to thank all of you for your emails, text messages, calls, meals, gifts, and prayers. But, please know that I am so completely thankful for each one of you!!!*

The final pathology report revealed that they removed my cancer in the nick of time. It was reclassified as "mass forming ductal carcinoma in situ." The doctor revealed that within six months, it would have been invasive. I sobbed that day, harder than I had when I had found out. This news meant I wouldn't have to endure chemo like so many others I would eventually meet. Like my friend in the chair I spoke with a couple months before.

Not one day has gone by in the nine years since my cancer diagnosis where I have not been thankful to the Lord that they found it in stage zero. Many people's stories do not end like mine. That same year, my sister lost one of her good friends to breast cancer at age thirty-three.

Soon after, it was time to recover and move on to reconstruction. The recovery process was brutal. I'll spare you the details, but it was truly a unique journey. It's important to note that I never took any pain medication and refused morphine during and after the surgery. I didn't realize at the time, but God would later show me my incessant need to feel pain. I had stood by for ten long years, watching Kate writhe in pain, vomiting, nausea, and mental anguish. I didn't want to numb myself and feel any reprieve that she hadn't been able to feel.

All I could think about after the double mastectomy was going back to running. Running. I needed to run. I needed to keep moving. Stuff the anxiety, feel the pain, then stuff the pain. I ignored doctor's orders, and just like after all my C-sections, I ran just three weeks after the double mastectomy.

My sister's double mastectomy was much more difficult than mine due to a different type of reconstruction. I was by her side and struggled greatly watching her try to navigate her pain. Her surgery was brutal. They cut large four-inch incisions in her back and removed muscles to use for her breast reconstruction. I cried often while watching the difficulty she endured.

We both moved on to reconstruction and eventually the ordeal ended. However, because of our gene mutation, we are required to have scans and blood work every six months until we remove all of our female organs, which is slated in the near future. I had to have several more abdominal surgeries to remove endometriosis and my fallopian tubes in an effort to prevent ovarian cancer. Multiple "-ectomies" occurred in a short duration of time. I realized then and even more now that God was slowly removing me and replacing *me* with Him.

Max Lucado's book title, *It's Not About Me,* was now imprinted in my soul.

***

My spiritual, personal, and health crises did not change the fact that our children still struggled, with one storm after another whipping through our lives.

Almost immediately after my surgeries were completed, Kate was diagnosed with whooping cough and ended up being sick for one hundred days. Appropriately, this illness is nicknamed "The 100 Day Cough." Despite being vaccinated, she had pertussis and succumbed to pneumonia four times during that time frame. I assumed the stress she was experiencing between her and my health issues was causing her mental breakdowns and psychotic episodes. She would ride a bipolar roller coaster of being angry, sad, and then completely collapsing in a pile of tears.

Education had become a tertiary thought with regards to Kate, and I knew this wasn't fair to her or to those who were not equipped to handle the challenges she was facing. Once she started having these psychotic episodes, we were forced to change schools and find a setting with educators who had experience teaching children with learning, mental health, and developmental struggles.

Bursts of anger flared during this season, but I never let the anger get control of me. I was able to return my thoughts to, "It's not about me." That statement became a centering mantra. It soothed my soul in every area except with running. Running continued to be a physical and emotional outlet for me. I didn't realize at the time, but that outlet was manifesting into an idol.

Much of my selfishness started to disappear. I was changing from the inside out. I transformed exponentially that year—a full mountaintop experience that lasted close to twelve months.

My physical body was undergoing -ectomies. Then, my spiritual awakening started with an "-ectomy." The "-ectomy" of me—the removal of the belief that my life was only about me or even my family. Now able to see how the Lord was using my circumstances and struggles, I grew closer to Him than ever before. For the first time, I could see purpose in all my suffering. I didn't just surrender. I accepted everything, and dare I say, found a reason to be thankful for it all.

After I recovered from the surgeries, people started referring women who had been diagnosed with breast cancer to me. I walked them through their journeys of surgeries, scans, and doctor appointments. It was the first time I saw my pain used for someone else's good. For my good. For God's glory. It brought me joy. Was this the good that God was referring to? It wasn't making me skinnier or prettier or wealthier. It was giving God glory because I was able to help these women understand the hope I had. I Peter 3:15. That was the verse He had given me that first night. Now I understand. It's not about me. There are people—many people—who God was going to help through my suffering.

After mountaintop experiences, we are never the same, but we do have to descend back into the valley. The valley of the shadow of death. I understood it wasn't about me. I understood my suffering had "good" purpose. But was I ready to completely die to all my self-interests? All of them?

# CHAPTER 8

## The Lightning Strike

Three years had passed since my breast cancer diagnosis. My struggles raged on and I had come off the mountaintop experience of seeing God use me straight into the valley of the shadow of death.

April 4, 2014 was the day that started my final descent into the death of self. I had been ignoring my hip pain for decades. In recent years I had been experiencing weakness in my left hip (likely due to the incessant running). By this point, I was running sixty miles per week. Inherently, I had an alignment issue with my hip. The years of relentlessly pounding the pavement finally took its toll on a beautiful spring day. I was running an intermittent hill repeatedly, followed by a moderate run of four miles.

During one of the hill repeats, I collapsed to the ground. When I stood up, I felt a sharp pain directly in my hip joint. In true Tiffany Haines fashion, I finished my run, limping but relentlessly completing what I set out to do that day.

After several more runs over a few more days, I realized this sharp pain felt more like bone pain. After googling all of my symptoms, I realized I may have a stress fracture. I made an appointment with my orthopedic doctor.

I begged him to do an MRI after he assured me there was no way I could have a fracture and still be running on my hip. He said no human could walk into the office with a fractured hip and not be in extreme pain, let alone run four miles. But he didn't know me. He didn't know I had learned how to run through the pain. He didn't know I lived with so many other kinds of pain, too. Contrarily, I knew my relentless will to fight at any cost and believed it was possible that I was running on a fractured hip. I won the "fight" for an MRI, and it was clear. Clear as in clearly fractured.

I received a call at 6:30 a.m. the next morning. It was the orthopedic surgeon urging me to get into the office as soon as it opened to get a pair of crutches. It was a serious fracture—on the femoral neck of the femur. It's an incredibly difficult bone to break. It's more common in older people with fragile bones, so he ordered a bone scan to make sure my bones weren't brittle. They weren't. They were strong.

This was not only a break of the femur but a break of my will. God knew running was the last idol to which I clung. He knew that in order to break my will, he had to allow my hip to break.

Genesis 32:24–25 says, "So Jacob was left alone, and a man wrestled with him until daybreak . . . he touched the socket of Jacob's hip so that his hip was wrenched as he wrestled with the man." **Jacob sported a limp for the rest of his life, and though my limp isn't physically evident, God did the same with me—both mentally and spiritually.**

The next eight weeks consisted of walking with crutches on a non-weight-bearing protocol. This meant I wasn't even allowed to touch my toe to the ground. With this restriction, my arms and right leg grew incredibly strong. My left leg atrophied. I will say that through all my surgeries and complications, this was one of the more difficult eight weeks I'd endured. I learned to carry things in creative ways and managed to take care of my children with only one leg.

Nevertheless, my iron-stone will, wrapped around this idol of running, made me more determined than ever to "survive and advance." While I had relented and given the rest of my storms to God, I could not bear the thought of relinquishing this demigod.

I never complained about my pain or circumstances, remaining stoic. This was representative of my life—just another trial, another storm, no big deal at this point. I was more determined than ever to get back at it, despite multiple warnings from doctors and therapists that I should never think about running again and needed to find a new outlet for my stress.

"No! I will prove them all wrong. I will run again at any cost, at all costs," I encouraged myself because my grip on my idol was steadfast. It was all I had left that I could control. My kids' health issues had spiraled completely out of control at this point. The hurricanes of relentless health crises were spawning tornadoes all around me.

I was still full of pride for one last thing—my will to defeat this particular storm. I no longer felt sad about the other storms around me. I no longer felt confused. I had accepted the pain of them. I even liked the pain. God was whispering for me to come all the way into the eye of the storm. He was inviting me to stop living in the eye wall. I didn't want to be ready, but this was the beginning of the end. My rebellion stemmed from the fact that I was used to the storms—maybe even addicted to them. The storms in my life had become my identity. I, rather cyn- ically, welcomed the pain. I enjoyed the fight. It felt like the ultimate race. The ultimate challenge. "Bring it. I'll

defeat it. Hit me again. Bruise me, break me, scar me."
This stubborn response became my survival mechanism.

Over the following year, I worked to regain enough muscle and strength to begin running again. I felt great. In some ways, I was the strongest (physically) I had ever been. I lifted weights and bolstered every muscle that needed to support my now fractured frame. However, what I didn't know is that metal screws and plates would be the only way my hips and knees would align properly.

I started running again after one year of rehab. Over the following year, I started running more than I ever had. The more I ran, the more I created stress, and the more destruction occurred within my knees.

God continued to prompt me to surrender. I still refused to reflect the sum of His glory. Sunlight was peeking through the dark clouds, but I refused to look—to give in to that last surrendering call.

Then it happened. My knee snapped. The lightning strike. The last blow. I was in a workout class, pushing myself to the edge, still believing the lie that my fight for control would last. The lady next to me watched me stumble to the ground. Within minutes, my kneecap was lost in an angry sea of inflammation. I could barely walk.

In my stubborn way, I took a week off and then kept running—running on a

> Bring it. I'll defeat it. Hit me again. Bruise me, break me, scar me.

destroyed knee and failing body. Even though I limped, I kept going. I couldn't walk up and down stairs without holding on to railings, and yet I ran. One day my physical therapist, who was still treating me for my hip, saw my grossly swollen knee.

"What are you doing? Have you gone mad?"

My orthopedic surgeon ordered another MRI, this time on my knee. My MCL was torn but there was a significant amount of inflammation and debris that needed to be attended to. My doctors recommended surgery as soon as possible. However, before scheduling the surgery, we headed off to a pre-planned vacation at the beach.

Strolling on the sand at the water's edge, I collapsed. A sharp pain shocked my bad knee, causing it to give out. I had experienced much pain in my life, but this was a full ten on the ten-point scale, nausea crashing my body like the waves in the ocean a few feet away. What else could have happened to my knee? Surgery was scheduled for late September.

\*\*\*

Also during this time, I was enduring multiple scans for ovarian cancer, breast cancer, undergoing treatment for iron deficiency—the list goes on. In addition, (as if anything else could be going on) my family was going through turmoil over a fractured friendship with another family. My life was filled with mediating the relationships between the families, then coming home to OCD, fear, anxiety, learning disabilities, sleepless nights, and my own pain and darkness. My health was failing and my only outlet, running, wasn't possible.

I was sitting directly in the eye wall of a major storm. The winds were at their highest speeds, the destruction from its relentless fury was now grossly evident. I often think of Chevy Chase in the movie, *Christmas Vacation,* when his family is begging him to release them—to allow them to leave to escape the hilariously horrid Christmas week of horrors. His character, Clark Griswold, blocks the door, and says, "Oh no, no one is leaving this good ole' fashioned family Christmas!"

To which his wife replies, "Everyone should go home Clark, in case this gets worse."

He replies, "Worse? How can it get worse? Look around Ellen, we are at the threshold of hel...!"

But it did get worse for the Griswold family, and it got worse for us, too.

At the same time our household was drowning in psychotic and spiritual crises, and while my knee was obliterated and I was awaiting surgery, my other doctors believed they had discovered a new growth in the reconstructed breast that had previously housed cancer. My storms were all upgraded to "Category 5." This new red-flag warning took precedence, and my knee surgery was rescheduled.

Then God reminded me of Angela. Remember Angela from sixth grade? All of a sudden, I became Angela. God showed me that I was always ready for a fight because the fight was easier.

I was raised in a white privileged home where I was told every single day that I could be whoever I wanted to be and do whatever I put my mind to. I was given money to dream and achieve and an education to accomplish those dreams.

In middle school, Angela didn't know where her next meal was coming from, who was going to love her, or when she would be free of her oppressive environment. For the first time, I was aligned with her. I understood survival. I understood pain. I understood Angela. She had been simply trying to survive, and the fight was all she knew. The fight was now all I knew. **I was Angela, and she was me.**

The week before my breast cancer exploratory surgery, all three of our children contracted a virus. Runny noses. Sore throats. I didn't even take them to the doctor since we were used to so much more. Little did I know, within this tri-

> All of a sudden, I became Angela. God showed me that I was always ready for a fight because the fight was easier.

ple-threat storm, God was about to unveil the answers we had been seeking for more than a decade.

I had just finished reading *The Weight of Glory* by C.S. Lewis. A "weighty" book with a profound message. I recommend every believer read Chapter One. It is the most powerful chapter in any book , with the exception of the Bible, I've ever read.

To paraphrase a few lines from the chapter, Lewis asks, "What if our entire life is supposed to be crushed and refined so that we bend our knees, raise our hands, and give Him glory . . . so that when we cross that line, His glory is bestowed upon us. And all of what we thought was wasted, is not."

This chapter led me to 2 Corinthians 4:17. "For our light and momentary troubles are achieving for us an eternal glory that far outweighs them all . . . " These words flamed my desire for God to transform my perspective and my life.

Meanwhile, the virus had worsened and terrorized our household. I wish I had cameras that captured the torture my children, Brad, and I experienced. Looking back, I believe it was purely demonic.

"For our light and momentary troubles are achieving for us an eternal glory that far outweighs them all ... " These words flamed my desire for God to transform my perspective and my life.

Kate started seeing people who were not there. At one point, she looked across our bedroom staring at what was invisible to us but visible to her. Satan was standing there.

"He's over there. He has a hole in his head and blood is pouring out."

One of our children was raging constantly, hitting me, spitting at me, running away from home. Constant anger, constant angst. One child stopped eating almost completely, losing weight by the day. Fear of throwing up, fear of sleeping, fear of going to school, fear of honestly everything.

I thought, "We need a priest!"

I was drowning in the absolute lowest point I had ever been. I was begging God to take all of our lives. "Please let us get hit by a truck on the highway. Take us home."

I just wanted the hurricanes to end. I was in agony. Oswald Chamber said it best in his book, *The Shadow of an Agony*:

> "Agony means severe suffering in which something dies—either the base thing, or the good. No man is the same after an agony; he is either better or worse, and the agony of a man's experience is nearly always the first thing

that opens the mind to understand the need of Redemption worked out through Jesus Christ . . . There is a frontier outside which Jesus Christ does not tell; but when once we get over that frontier, He becomes our all in all."

Agony. We were living in agony. When Oswald Chambers said that 'something dies, either the base thing or the good' he meant that either our will dies or our hope. I was now at the edge of the moral frontier. I was willing to cross the line of moral solitude in order to survive. I saw my true need for Redemption. A Savior. Lightning had struck.

\*\*\*

I underwent the first surgery to investigate the suspected tumor at the beginning of October. Our kids were still acting insane. I couldn't walk. Our family was being torn apart. These hurricanes rendered me defenseless—well past my capacity to function wholly or live through anything else.

The "tumor" ended up being an issue from my previous reconstructive surgery, not cancer. However, I had to have a complete reconstruction of both breasts once again. I limped away with twenty-six different incisions—my body black and blue—but still cancer-free. My whole body throbbed with pain from my chest down to my knee.

My knee surgery was scheduled a month later in November. The surgeon suspected a tibial plateau fracture and warned me I would be in a wheelchair following surgery. I couldn't imagine how I would be a mom to our children from a wheelchair!

After surgery, the diagnosis sounded less catastrophic, but the future function of my knee was in limbo.

"How have you been running?" the surgeon asked when I woke up from the anesthesia. "You literally have no cartilage left in your knee. You have Grade 4 arthritis, and your knee is destroyed." I wouldn't admit it then, but the "-ectomy" of cartilage was the nail in the coffin for my running.

Miscommunication between the doctor and the nurse resulted in no one telling me I should be on crutches when discharged. I walked out of the hospital unassisted as Brad went to retrieve the car from the parking lot.

A day later, I turned to Brad. "I've had twelve major surgeries. But I'm having post-surgical pain like no other. Something is wrong."

We couldn't see the toes on my foot. Brad immediately recognized compartment syndrome and called the doctor.

"Why is she walking?" the doctor asked incredulously. "She should be on crutches! And by the way, she will never run again."

Brad didn't tell me that second part. He knew how much it would crush my spirit. My mom took me back to the doctor so he could pull out the fluid, which had filled my knee. There wasn't time to numb me, and I didn't move when he jabbed the giant syringes into my leg. I didn't even blink.

The doctor stared at me. "What have you been through? I'm about to retire. I've never seen anyone who didn't even flinch to extract fluid like this."

I stared at the wall, feeling dead inside.

My mom asked, "Why do you ask?"

The doctor explained that only twice in his thirty years in practice had he come across pain tolerance like mine. "Both times, the emotional pain my patients were experiencing was more than the physical pain. What have you been through?"

My mom simply replied, "A lot."

I was stoic. "When can I run again?"

The doctor quickly replied, "Tiffany, *you can never run again.*"

I was Jacob wrestling with the angel, except everyone else seemed to clearly understand that running wouldn't exist in my future. I sought out second and third opinions, looking for something to grab hold of—a buoy of sorts. Someone who could tell me there was a chance I could keep running. No one did. My idol of running was finally and completely stripped away. I left on crutches once again.

Death. Over the years, I had been diagnosed with cancer, fought to raise a child who is developmentally delayed and may never leave my household, and my kids have so many diagnoses I could write a psychiatry book. But being told I couldn't run . . . *that* was devastating. It was the only thing I had left that was "mine." It was the last grip on what I believed was the only thing that controlled my anxiety. God wanted to control my anxiety. He had always wanted to but I hadn't let Him. Until now.

Finally, after years of wrestling, I waved the white flag.

In a devotional blog post called, "Do You Walk in White?" Oswald Chambers, Author of *My Utmost for His Highest*, writes about the death of self.

> "Death means you stop being. You must agree with God and stop being the intensely striving kind of Christian you have been. We avoid the cemetery and continually refuse our own death. It will not happen by striving, but by yielding to death.'" (Romans 6:3)

I was ready to surrender. I had no will left. I had nothing left. No fight, no strength, no health, no research, no running . . . nothing. I had nothing to give Him but me. ALL OF ME. We refuse to die to self because of Genesis 3. Satan turned the mirror on us. He tricked us into thinking that living for God's glory is boring. He convinced us that death to self leads to unhappiness, when in fact it is *only through* death to self that we can experience true joy.

In *The Shadow of an Agony,* Oswald Chambers also wrote, "Redemption does not amount to anything to a man until he meets an agony; until that time he may have been indifferent; but knock the bottom board out of his wits, bring him to the limit of his moral life, produce the supreme suffering worthy of the name agony, and he will begin to realize that there is more in Redemption than he had ever dreamed, and it is at that phase that he is prepared to hear Jesus say, 'Come unto Me.' Our Lord said, I did not call the man who is all right; I came to call the man who is at his wits' end, the man who has reached the moral frontier.'" It was helpful for me to know that others had been to the edge too. It's a real place. Jesus tells us that the people who find themselves on this ethical boundary line are the people He came to save.

On November 1, 2016, I acquiesced everything to God, including my ability to run. I was at the threshold of the underworld. This would be the last "-ectomy."

I texted my sisters.

> *Pray for me. I don't think I can take much more.*

When I succumbed, the sunlight came through the black clouds.

As God had already put in motion, I was scheduled to speak at a women's ministry event the following day. I told the crowd that His glory was His highest priority, and it was now mine as well. I told this group of women that I could see myself walking into heaven and feeling the warmth of His glory bestowed upon me. I saw my need for redemption. I saw the darkest parts deep inside me. I saw my ability to cross the moral frontier and commit any sin on this earth. But I also saw Jesus hanging on the cross, and I saw the little girl version of me in church that didn't think she was a wretch. That day, I knew I needed God more than ever. Just then, God grabbed my hand and said, "Come to me those who are heavy laden."

The very next morning the phone rang. It was my sister, Kathryn. Since my desperate text, she had been praying for me feverishly. Everyone close to me was. They knew I couldn't take much more. I barely got out a *hello*.

"Tiffany, I know what your kids have! They have PANS—"

# CHAPTER 9

# PANS and the Problem with Pain

My sister had a good friend who seemed to have endured a similar fate with her daughter. As my sister told her friend about what my children had been experiencing, the woman tearfully looked her in the eyes and said, "Your sister's kids . . . they have PANS."

In a blink of an eye, the multi-year mystery was over. This woman—an angel sent from God—knew a PANS specialist in Washington D.C. Two weeks after my sister's call, Brad and I flew two of our kids to the specialist in Washington to be evaluated.

PANS stands for pediatric acute-onset neuropsychiatric syndrome. It is a subset of PANDAS (pediatric acute neuropsychiatric disorder associated with strep)—those whose brain inflammation trigger is strep. It is a syndrome that causes brain inflammation. Bacterial infections, viral infections, allergies, and even stress are among many triggers of the inflammation. It most often occurs suddenly—like a tornado with no warning. However, it can happen over time and most parents will notice warning signs in hindsight. It abruptly hits, just like the hurricanes that have occurred throughout my life. Treatment is complex and can include antibiotics, anti-virals, IVIG (intravenous immunoglobulin therapy), various immunosuppressants, as well as various natural therapies. Most will try every version of therapy at one point in the journey.

Believed to be an autoimmune condition, PANS affects an estimated one in 200 kids. Personally, I believe more are affected. In my opinion, many diagnoses such as ADD (attention deficit disorder), Tourette's syndrome, and childhood OCD (obsessive-compulsive disorder) can be attributed to PANS. I like to think of PANS as synonymous with brain inflammation.

Both of our children were diagnosed with PANS. Our third child was diagnosed several months later. They each had several different infections raging in each of their bodies. The doctor prescribed specific antibiotics. I couldn't believe the answers were finally coming.

Within just a few months, two of our children began to make incredible improvements. They started sleeping, stopped arguing, and stopped raging, hitting, and spitting. The OCD, though still present, was markedly improved. Academically they improved—especially in math.

Understanding PANS not only explained all of their odd behaviors, but, for the first time, validated my concerns. With all of my research, why had I never come across this diagnosis? Why did none of the dozens of specialists know of this disorder? While questions plagued my mind, I was incredibly relieved that we finally had a diagnosis. Better yet, a diagnosis, that while there is no cure, there is treatment.

This may seem like the ending, right? We have a diagnosis with treatment. We have an answer—finally, at long last. God was standing right next to me in the darkness all along. However, this darkness, at least on earth, does not have a perfect ending. PANS, as anyone who has endured it knows, is a winding road. **A winding, thorny road with twists and turns that cannot be predicted.** While I have never returned to the exact same darkness that I once experienced, I assure you I am still in the valley of the shadow of death.

PANS defines "death of self." It forces it. It causes pain and PTSD that only those who've experienced its war understand. Pain is a difficult issue in the world of PANS and other special needs. The human psyche can only take so much trauma until an internal defense mechanism kicks in, and we figure out a new way to survive. Survival becomes a daily strategy. We find ways to numb our pain. I have mentioned the basketball term "Survive and Advance" often because I assure you, many of us in this world live this way every day.

Survive the episode, advance to the next episode. Survive one treatment, advance to the next. Survive the fear of never being able to see your child be free of the nightmare, advance to the fear of losing them once they return to normalcy. Survive the poor reaction we had toward our child, advance to the next poor reaction. I can't tell you how many times I have prayed to God that He would blot my words or reactions from my children's memories.

We are constantly at the edge of the moral frontier. We are at the end of our ropes almost daily. The pain of hopelessness of not having answers and having no efficient help from doctors and specialists breeds a spiral of isolation and

> PANS defines "death of self." It forces it. It causes pain and PTSD that only those who've experienced its war understand.

depression that is, at times, impossible to describe unless you have been through it. Some numb the pain with alcohol and drugs. Some dive into depression. All the same, we have found ways to cope with daily trauma that is PANS and special needs.

I seem to have taken the path of wanting and needing to feel physical pain because of the emotional numbness I felt as a result of so much trauma. In my case, I never created the physical pain, but by happenstance, endured multiple surgeries and injuries.

Looking back, I felt more alive when I felt physical pain, especially when I couldn't take it away from my children. Once my physical afflictions were healed, I took on the pain other PANS and special needs families were experiencing. I couldn't fix my kids, but I found relief in fixing other people's heartbreak by helping them name and understand PANS. It became an unhealthy spiral where I piled on more and more of others' burdens, which I truly couldn't handle.

As I write this book, the Holy Spirit is revealing these unhealthy coping mechanisms to me. I often feel like I must hold others' burdens myself. It's a mentality I thought I had shed: "If we don't research, we won't find the answer. If we don't supplement correctly, they won't get better. If we don't fight hard enough, they won't survive." These are lies fed by the enemy. Jesus asks us throughout scripture to invite Him into the pain.

Let Him take our burdens. Let Him bring us answers. We will remain in the eye wall permanently if we don't grasp this concept. We have to learn, no matter how traumatic, no matter how damaging the turmoil, that He loves our children more than we do. That only He is capable of bearing their pain and their trauma. That only He holds the perfect ending.

Today, I have been asking God to take my pain. To enter in and carry it. I write this after walking through a severe episode with our son. A few weeks ago, he had a virus that produced a cough. It seemed simple enough. But that simple cough caused brain inflammation, which superseded prophylactic antibiotics, countless supplements, and two types of anti-inflammatories. Our son has been angry, sad, and delusional. Last night—out of the blue—he started fearing that I was going to kill him. Screeching in terror, he ran from me as if I was a murderer. I had become an intruder in our home. I gently reached out to him, trying to love him.

"You are a nightmare!" he screamed as my approach terrified him.

As a mom, this was heart wrenching. We love our children more than anything. I would literally die for him, and yet his psychosis caused him to fear that I would not die, but kill. There is no worse moment for a mom. Our brains can't take the pain of it, so it naturally dulls the sharpness of the moment. Last night, I was in a crowded room full of noise, yet I felt silence. I felt darkness in a room full of light. That is PANS. I wonder how long we will have to wait for answers. I wonder how long it will take specialists and doctors and scientists to secure enough money to accomplish the needed research. I wonder if we will lose our children to suicide or lives full of depression and never-ending OCD symptoms.

But then I remembered—at the moment I was reaching out to love my son, there was God who did much more. He sent His Son to die for that moment. That day. This day. This pain. This burden.

I remembered that the darkness of this disease cannot penetrate the glory of the cross. On that cross lay this day full of pain. It's already been paid for. It has been swallowed in victory. The enemy of this world can't touch the miracle of that day. All at once, the cross numbs my pain—this time in a healthy way. A glorious way. My burden feels lighter even though the sting of suffering is evident on my weary body.

> "For our light and momentary troubles are achieving for us an eternal glory that far outweighs them all." (2 Corinthians 4:17)

I write this book because in the PANS and special needs world, heaven and the promise of Glory is often all we have as motivation to continue. We are not guaranteed healing on this earth. We are not guaranteed an end to our suffering on this earth. We are not guaranteed the answers we so desperately seek. But as believers, we are guaranteed that His glory—*His approval*—will at last be bestowed upon a world where darkness cannot penetrate the light. We will enter a world where there is *only* hope. We will enter a world where depression, OCD, and anxiety *cannot* exist. We will finally, at long last, sit at Jesus' feet and see from His perspective why we experienced so much suffering, and it will indeed be good. His Glory, His acceptance of us is best described by C.S. Lewis: "For glory means good report with God, acceptance by God, response, acknowledgement, and welcome into the heart of things. The door on which we have been knocking all our lives will open at last."

Today, I rest in some of the final verses of Revelation. They give me peace and hope that one day, mine and our children's suffering will not only end, but will have a grand purpose that will have made it all worth it.

"Then the angel showed me the river of the water of life, as clear as crystal, flowing from the throne of God and of the Lamb down the middle of the great street of the city. On each side of the river stood the tree of life, bearing twelve crops of fruit, yielding its fruit every month. And the leaves of the tree are for the **healing** of the nations. No longer will there be any curse. The throne of God and of the Lamb will be in the city, and his servants will serve him. They will **see his face**, and his name will be on their foreheads. There will be no more night. They will not need the light of a lamp or the light of the sun, for the Lord God will give them light. And they will reign for ever and ever." (Revelation 22:1–5, bold added for emphasis)

I can't wait to see His face. Then healing will be complete. And *this* day will become glory.

# CHAPTER 10

## Kate

Now that we know the root diagnosis, I want to share a unique perspective from Kate's view. Kate has a simple faith. She has always seen God with a pure heart. She loves Him. She loves Him in a way that makes me marvel. She may lack intelligence as the world views intelligence, but her ability to love and worship Jesus is well beyond her years. She regularly listens to worship music. It is her only relief. I once asked her why she loves Jesus so much, and

I once asked her why she loves Jesus so much, and she replied simply, as if there shouldn't exist another answer, "Because mom, He is all I have."

she replied simply, as if there shouldn't exist another answer, "Because mom, He is all I have."

Kate has been plagued with mental illness, which I now believe was brought on by PANS. She was born into mental anguish and will die in mental anguish, barring a significant shift in our current reality. She is imprisoned in a world of OCD, fear, and anxiety. She has never known one day without these struggles. Not one. She has been consumed with night terrors, cyclical vomiting, nausea, dizziness, severe abdominal pain, joint pain, and complete mental pain. Every event registers as trauma for her. Every circumstance swirls in her world of OCD. A great analogy is the art piece, "Relativity" by M. C. Escher, which depicts a never-ending staircase. That is her mind.

Every event is a storm (and I mean EVERY thunderstorm, tornado threat, or hurricane—a nod to the name of my book). Every test, bath, hair wash, haircut, new outfit (she wears the same thing every day), relationship, school day, field trip, vacation, night she has to be separated from me in her bed by herself, crowded building, store, or church she has ever walked into registers as trauma in her mind. Yes, even church—especially church—is traumatizing for her. There are too many loud noises, too many people, too much chaos. And fear for us both.

"What will they say?

What will they require of us?

Will I feel like a failure?

Will they understand her anxiety?

Will they see her mind entangled in the web of fear and anxiety?"

These are the thoughts Kate's fears and struggles trigger in me, creating my own trauma-based response. Imagine watching your child endure this every day. Imagine the pain we have felt not being able to free her from this pain. Countless counselors and specialists, over thirty different medications, occupational therapy, speech therapy, music therapy, hyperbaric oxygen treatments, neuro-therapy, every supplement known to man, B12 shots, a gluten free diet, a dairy free diet, chelation, neurologists, immunologists, gastroenterologists, neuro scientists, psychologists, psychiatrists, and I could continue. She has been diagnosed with PANS, anxiety disorder, obsessive-compulsive disorder, mood disorder, mast cell activation syndrome, and sensory processing disorder—just to name a few.

But Jesus. Her only relief is Jesus. That's it. He's all she has and He's all I have for her. But He is enough. The pain of not being able to stop her pain is unbearable for me. I cry as I write this. But He can carry her burden and He can carry mine. These are a few stories that I want to share about Kate, an incredible child held close by a loving God.

\*\*\*

He started appearing to Kate when she was three years old. She has never slept well and never wakes up rested. But one day at age three, she bounded out of bed, telling me she had encountered angels.

"Mommy, God let me meet angels last night! I was so scared, and they came into my room and took me on a ride in the sky. They had white clothing that was so bright, Mommy!! They played toys with me. I wasn't scared anymore when they brought me home."

When Kate was ten, she woke up next to me one morning, and her eyes were filled with light. It is difficult to explain, but they shone brighter than I had ever seen them. Kate's eyes often look dark and lifeless but they now looked like she had just seen Jesus.

"Mom, I went to heaven last night. God took me there and our whole family was there. It was so beautiful. There were colors I had never seen. We watched movies about how all of our lives were connected. God showed us how He is in control of our lives, and now I truly believe in heaven. I can't wait to go there, Mom, It's amazing!"

As I've mentioned, Kate has struggled with cyclical vomiting syndrome for years. She has always had chronic panic attacks, and they would cause her to vomit. Her anxiety is so severe, she would often vomit daily, and sometimes, it would be so bad that she would vomit for hours—upwards of four to five days per week. Her school would call me if they couldn't stop her from vomiting, and I would have to pick her up (thankfully Mast Cell Activation treatment has now cured this symptom).

One day when she was fifteen, the school called and mentioned she was starting to throw up, and I should be on call if they couldn't stop it. Miraculously, I never received a return call and didn't have to pick her up early.

That night, she was in the bath (I still have to help her wash her hair) and said, "Mom, you have to hear what happened to me today. Did the school call you and tell you I was having a panic attack? It was amazing, Mom. I was sitting there and all the teachers were trying to calm me down. I felt my skin crawling and my anxiety rising, and I was about to throw up. Then, I saw Jesus sitting on the board. I've seen him before. I can never see his face, but he wears bright white clothes. It's a white we don't have here on Earth. It's so bright you can barely look at Him. He has long hair. I heard him whispering to me. I knew the only way I could hear His voice was to calm down. My teachers thought they were calming me, but I so badly wanted to hear His voice. As I calmed down and stopped crying, His voice got louder and louder, and it sounded like booming thunder!! Except, I wasn't scared of this thunder. It was calming. I looked around wondering if others could hear it, but I already knew they couldn't. God gave me verse after verse—"

Kate proceeded to recite Scripture passages (though she had never learned them).

"Then he showed me a number. Mom, you know how I don't understand numbers? Well, I did at that moment!! He told me it was the number of prayers He had answered for me. Then he showed me another number. It was the number of prayers He still had yet to answer for me. Then he told me this was not my home. My home is in heaven where I will be whole. I won't be afraid, and I won't fear. He told me He loves me so much. Now I know heaven exists. The rest of the day I have felt peace."

Kate still talks about this story to this day. She wishes she could remember the numbers because she says they were really big. I find tremendous comfort in this story. It reminds me that He loves her so much more than I do or even can. It reminds me that we have to be still to hear His voice. It reminds me how any child of God can hear His big thundering voice if we just remember to be quiet enough to listen. It reminds me that though she is the 'least of these' on this earth, God has a wonderful place ready for her in heaven. I long for heaven. For her. For me. For everyone. It is the only place where I know she will be free.

# CHAPTER 11

## Understanding the Eternal Weight of Glory

The human race is in its own inflammatory condition. Much like with PANS, it's wreaking havoc in our personal, relational, and spiritual lives. It seems counter-cultural or counter-intuitive to give up our lives for God. But our intuition is wrong. Our souls will be empty if we're not living out our godly purpose.

Throughout my trauma, I have learned to study and embrace the logic of God. We have to understand the beginning to understand the ending.

## Created for God's Glory

1. First, we were created uniquely and purposefully for the glory of God (Isaiah 34:7). We were created in the image of His glory and for His glory (Genesis 1:27). We must understand this premise first, before understanding anything that follows. If we were crafted, designed, and formed for His glory, then will living for ourselves make us happy? No. We can argue this, we can deny it, we can debate it. The fact remains, if you believe God's written word, you also have to believe we were created for His glory.

## Entrance of Sin - The Mirror Turns Away from God and Turns Toward Us

2. So, if this is true, why don't we follow this? In Genesis 3, we were living in the Garden of Eden, free of sin, enjoying God's creation, bathed in the image of His Glory. Then Satan came along and said, wait did He say it's all about Him? *No, it's about you*! He twisted God's words and turned the mirror away from reflecting God's glory and turned the mirror on us. And we have believed that lie ever since. His lie made us believe that *our good* was the ultimate prize.

Why are we so quick to assume that if we pray enough, go to church enough, and commit enough benevolent acts that we will be blessed? It's simply because as a church and as a society we have believed the lie that it's all about our glory, our kingdom building and *our good*. But do we understand what good means?

Our definition of good is defined by our finite view of what we see as blessings on earth. Romans 8:28 says, "And we know that in all things God works for the good of those who love him, who have been called according to his purpose."

In my opinion, we use this verse to assure ourselves that we will be blessed with what we find to be good—health, beauty, intelligence, safety, or wealth. Satan's lure is to make us think it's "good" for ourselves that can be achieved. Sadly, this is a ghost we can chase but will never capture. We will never be wealthy enough, smart enough, accomplished

In my opinion, we use this verse to assure ourselves that we will be blessed with what we find to be good—health, beauty, intelligence, safety, or wealth.

enough, or skinny enough. Satan knows this. He watches and enjoys the chase.

## God Uses All Things

3. Romans 8:28 specifically mentions that God works in *all things*. "All things" refers to *all* things—good and bad, celebrations and trials, tribulations and joyful experiences. It's important to know that God uses all things for His glory, which will in turn produce humility, character, and knowledge of our need for the cross of Christ. This is *good*. The end game isn't more money, a better job, or more successful children. There is never enough perfection. We can't achieve it.

## For Our Good, God Defines Glory

4. God can't transfer His glory to us here on earth. Isaiah 42:8 says, "I am the Lord; that is My name! I will not give My glory to another or My praise to idols." He doesn't do this because if He did, it would be all about us. If it's all about us, then the weight of the world is on OUR shoulders. He is the alpha and the omega, the beginning and the end. He IS glory. He defines it and we need Him to retain ownership of that glory. We don't want that responsibility.

## Suffering is an Essential Part of Kingdom Building

5. Romans 8:29 and 8:36 says, "For those God foreknew He also predestined to be conformed to the image of His Son, that He might be firstborn among many brothers and sisters. And those He predestined, He also called; those He called, He also justified; those He justified, He also glorified. As it is written: For your sake we face death all day long; we are considered as sheep to be slaughtered."

So again, if our purpose is defined as glorifying God because this is the way the universe was crafted, created, and ordered, then it's also important to know that He chose us to be afflicted, facing death all day long, ready to be slaughtered. Though this sounds drastic, **His purpose is for our *self-interest* to be destroyed so that we may carry out His purpose of helping others.**

Our purpose here on earth is to partake in the sufferings of Christ and become more like Jesus so that we may nurture, support, and love the future kingdom of heaven. This is what brings us joy. This is good. Good for God's glory and good for us.

## The Ending - Glory Bestowed

6. If we must understand the beginning—which is that we were born, crafted, and created for His glory—then we must also understand the end. Revelation 22 is entitled, "*Eden Restored.*"

"Then the angel showed me the river of the water of life, as clear as crystal, flowing form the Throne of God and the Lamp down to the middle of the great street of the city. On each side of the river stood the tree of life, bearing twelve crops of fruit, yielding its fruit every month. The leaves of the tree are for the healing of the nations. No longer will there be any curse . . . And they will reign forever and ever."

There was once a garden where two trees were offered. In this last restored Eden there will only be one. You see, God knew we would pick the wrong tree. He knew we would suffer. He knew we would sin. He knew.

He also knew there was another Eden—a new Eden with only one tree. He knew that—just as with the greatest movie you have ever seen—there was an ending that would make all of our suffering worth it. He knew our suffering would show us our need for the cross of Christ. It was the plan all along.

Most importantly, He knew that He would bestow glory upon us. C.S. Lewis defines glory as, "fame with God, approval or (I might say) 'appreciation' by God . . . a child before his teacher, a creature before its Creator . . . and this is enough to raise our thoughts to what may happen when the redeemed soul, beyond all hope and nearly beyond all belief, learns at last that she has pleased Him whom she was created to please. There will be no more room for vanity then. She will be free from the miserable illusion that is her doing. With no taint of what we should now call self-approval she will most innocently rejoice in the thing God has made her to be, and the moment that heals her old inferiority complex forever. **If God is satisfied with the work, the work may be satisfied with itself.**"

C.S. Lewis mentions that what we truly seek is God's approval and that "glory bestowed" meant approval from God. After recognizing this he says, "With that, a good deal of what I had been thinking all my life fell down like a house of cards." We spend our lives seeking everyone's approval when in reality it is our Creator's acceptance that we truly seek. C.S. Lewis concludes in the *The Weight of Glory*, "The promise of glory is the promise, almost incredibly and only possible by the work of Christ, that some of us, that any of us who really chooses shall actually survive that examination, shall find approval, shall please God. To please God . . . to be loved by God, not merely pitied, but delighted in as an artist delights in His work or a father in a son—it seems impossible, a weight or burden of glory which our thoughts can hardly sustain. But so it is."

Today, I am deep into PANS research—helping others on their parenting journeys. I counsel other parents, guiding them and encouraging them on a very dark journey.

*My life isn't about me,* and thank the Lord above it isn't. It is about God's glory, and this is how I have the opportunity to impact His Kingdom. I had to go through everything I did to truly understand this truth and to put away my idols. To stop trying to run the fastest race. To stop trying to fix everyone. To stop striving to be the perfect mom and the perfect Christian. I can't carry my children's burden or anyone else's for that matter. Only Jesus can. Only Jesus did. That day on the Cross.

The storms still rage. PANS doesn't just go away. Despite a popular belief circulating in our culture, parenting children with special needs doesn't get easier with time. There are ups and downs. Sometimes more downs than ups. I still shake my fist at God on occasion. I am human.

This truth, however, reigns in my life. My joy is helping others. My joy is recognizing that there is purpose to my pain. Your pain. You have an amazing story too. One that God is waiting to use for His purpose. The grand purpose of cheering on others in the race. They are tired, weary, and injured. They need you to reach out in this race of life, hand them living water, and pass the baton.

One day the race will be over and the last person will cross the finish line. The wounds of our suffering will be healed. The memory of our pain will be beautifully crafted into glory. As we cross that finish line, our faces glowing, a loud thundering voice will say, "Well done my good and faithful servant." Finally, at long last, Kate will be free of her shackles, as will our other children. Our inferiority complex will be healed at long last with the kiss of GLORY.

# *Postlude*

As I concluded the writing of this book, I had another dream. In this dream, after enduring some type of war, I stood on top of the earth with two men. Innately in this dream, I knew that the two men couldn't see me, as they were representative of the conscious in my mind. They were the dichotomy found in all of us.

The question was presented, though not verbally, whether or not I would give God glory or whether I would chase my own. The man on the right was relatively certain that he would give God glory but was waffling in his decision. The other man on the left was the dominant personality and immediately interrupted the other man's thoughts and stated, "Of course we will give God glory. He is glory. The glory is His."

With this decision, another man appeared. I knew this man was given as a gift for the decision I had just made. He had no eyes. I also knew this man was Faith. He immediately took my hand, and I shrunk down to a child. My mind was still in its adult consciousness, but I looked like a child. Then this third man put me on his shoulders and carried me through a beautiful path that looked like how I envision the Garden of Eden. I began to cry as we walked down the path. Though this man had no eyes, he could clearly see where he was taking me.

I was mourning the pain I had from the suffering. I was releasing it while he was carrying me down the path. Finally, I felt relief. Without words, this man with no eyes was comforting me.

I knew he, Faith, was leading me to the Kingdom of Heaven and showing me the Kingdom of God. I knew, in those moments, all of my pain was worth it. I knew at the end of this path lie a beautiful explanation for my pain.

*** 

I end with this dream because I'm certain God gave it to me as I concluded the book for two very important reasons.

Throughout the past eighteen years, I have realized it's not about me. That is good. That is the way it should be. I've decided to give God glory for whatever path

God lays before me. I can't add to his glory, as He is the essence of its definition. This glory is rightfully his and for *our* good.

Once I chose to give Him glory and stop chasing my own, a wonderful gift was given to me. The gift of Faith. The man had no eyes because he has no need for eyes. Faith is defined in Hebrews 11:1, "Now faith is the substance of things hoped for, the evidence of things not seen." (KJV)

The man with no eyes knew where he was taking me. He was a gift because that faith would lead me to the Kingdom of Heaven. My tears, my pain, my suffering—it's all worth it. I knew we were headed to the Kingdom of Heaven, but I hadn't yet received the promise. In fact, I woke up before reaching Heaven. Why? Because I still have work to do.

**We must be faithful while not yet receiving our promise.** Hebrews 11:13, says, "All these people were still living by faith when they died. They did not receive the things promised; they only saw them and welcomed them from a distance, admitting they were foreigners and strangers on earth."

I don't belong here. I am a foreigner in a strange land. Faith will take me with all my scars and all my tears to a far-away land where those scars and tears will be sealed with glory.

# A Note about *PANS* and *PANDAS*

PANS, or pediatric acute-onset neuropsychiatric syndrome, is an autoimmune condition caused by infections. Research indicates PANS can be triggered by numerous infections, including Borrelia burgdorferi (Lyme disease), mycoplasma pneumonia, herpes simplex, the common cold virus, influenza (particularly H1N1), and other viruses.

PANDAS is a disorder associated with only streptococcal infections—specifically group A strep. Although the etiology for PANS is different from PANDAS, the symptoms are nearly identical and include anxiety, motor tics, irritability, hyperactivity, sleep disturbances, sudden onset of obsessive-compulsive disorder (OCD), irrational fears, mood swings, anorexia, and urinary problems.

Parents and medical professionals alike agree that obtaining a correct diagnosis is challenging because the symptoms can mimic other illnesses. Children with PANS and PANDAS are often misdiagnosed as having a mental illness and are prescribed psychiatric drugs to help manage their symptoms. Unfortunately, this does not address the root cause of the symptoms, which is an infection-triggered autoimmune condition.

> *"Parents will describe children with PANS as overcome by a 'ferocious' onset of obsessive thoughts, compulsive rituals, and overwhelming fears. Clinicians should consider PANS when children or adolescents present with such acute-onset of OCD or eating restrictions in the absence of a clear link to strep."*
> —Dr. Susan Swedo, NIMH

When given appropriate treatment, patients with PANS and PANDAS can experience complete symptom resolution, or their symptoms are at least significantly reduced. This is the reason an early and accurate diagnosis and continuing research is critical to the quality of life and functional capabilities of these patients and their families.[1]

---

1  "What is PANS?" Moleculera Labs. https://www.moleculeralabs.com/what-is-pans/.

# An Open Letter to Parents

Dear parents of children with PANS or other special needs,

I want to say that I love you without knowing you. I feel your pain. I see your heart that has been torn in a thousand pieces over and over. I see the "thankless" job that you do every day. I know that tomorrow you will get up and do it again while being told what a horrible mom you are, while they spit at you and kick you, and tell you how worthless you are. But I know your worth. I know what every Mother's Day feels like when you just want your child(ren) to appreciate what you've done for them, yet they can't comprehend its brevity.

I know that you deserve a Ph.D. in medicine, critiquing scientific journals, homeopathy, and any other controversial topic regarding your child(ren)'s health. I know how it feels to watch the other siblings suffer and cry and watch the trauma unfold, knowing it will affect them for the rest of their lives. I know what it feels like to see a thousand specialists, and yet have no one have an answer as to how to help them. I know the suffocation of watching your child slip away, and I know the suffocation of seeing your child return and fear them slipping away again. I know the PTSD you feel every time you see a picture of the vacation or event that went awry because of their condition. I know the PTSD of fearing the next rage or the next time they stop eating. I know the pain of watching your child not be able to walk in school without paralyzing fear. I know the PTSD of fearing they won't walk in school after they did the day before. I know what it feels like when family, in-laws, teachers, and caregivers look at you like your child is crazy and like *you* are crazy. For those teachers and caregivers who have cared deeply, you have no idea our appreciation and you will have crowns in heaven!!

I know what it feels like to be humiliated. I know what it feels like to love your child in completion, but hate the disease so deeply that the lines are blurred between your child and the hate you have for its darkness. I know what it feels like to get up every day and fight the fight all over again with no answers despite a thousand articles read, too many specialists seen, and a million drugs and supplements taken.

But there is One who does know the answers. There is One who holds every tear in His jars. There is One who is going to use you. There is One who will make a pathway in the wilderness. He loves you more than I do. He will use your pain as someone else's survival guide. He is doing something new. Don't you see it?

> "Forget the former things; do not dwell on the past. See, I am doing a new thing! Now it springs up; do you not perceive it? I am making a way in the wilderness and streams in the wasteland." (Isaiah 43:18-19)

In love,
Tiffany

# An Open Letter to the Church

Dear Church,

Oftentimes, when meeting with parents of children with PANS or other special needs, I find that most are frustrated with the "Church." They feel abandoned and rejected by the Church. They feel the Church doesn't care for or recognize the children who don't fit in some predefined box. Instead, they feel judged and excluded by the very people they expect to love them. Before I continue, please know that my intention is not to put the Church on trial, but to start a conversation about how to change the current narrative.

Going to church has been and continues to be difficult for our family. My child with special needs has sensory issues, which prevent her (and us) from attending church. Church participation for all of my children—with their anxiety—has been difficult because of the inconsistent nature of rotating teachers and children. This is a common thread throughout the special needs and PANS world.

Even Christian schools often don't have programs or services for these kids. I was at odds as to why this is true. I found there are three main reasons. Number one, the "Church" is fallible, just as we are. Meaning, we are humans and sinners, as are all those who make up the Church. Number two, we often conform to the theology of our denomination as opposed to conforming to the image of Jesus. And finally, churchgoers' hearts are often good, but they simply don't know what to do or don't feel they have the resources to provide for children with significant special needs.

We live in an ordered society, which is good in so many ways, but it often promotes the idea of creating an environment for the people who "fit in the box," per say. Churches often create a budget that provides for women's ministries, men's ministries, children's ministries, mission opportunities, and divorce care. But we forget that twenty percent of U.S. households have an individual with special needs in the home. We forget this because those same families often don't attend church because their child can't handle the sensory environment of church, can't sit still in an ordered classroom, and don't integrate well with other children because of anxiety, fear, or other challenges.

We often operate within the confines of what feels comfortable and calm. However, Jesus got his hands dirty. He cared for the prostitute, the destitute, and the diseased. I, too, am guilty of staying in my comfort zone, but as I've navigated the PANS/special needs world, I've learned the more I study the character of Jesus, the more I get my hands dirty. The more I listen, the less I judge. The more I suffer, the more I care for the suffering. I love getting my hands dirty now. I love it because I know life isn't always pretty and neatly tied together with a shiny bow.

I'm simply asking the Church to get in the trenches with us. In conforming to His image and learning more about Jesus himself. Avoid doing what other institutions do or don't do—Jesus gives us the guideline as to how we should treat "the least of these."

God gave us the two highest commands in a specific order. The Great Commandment needs to be applied every day, in every situation, and in every institution that follows Christ's principles. Matthew 22:36–40 says, "Teacher, which is the greatest commandment in the Law? Jesus replied; 'Love the Lord your God with all your heart with all your soul and with all your mind. This is the first and greatest commandment. And the second is like it: Love your neighbor as yourself. All the Law and the Prophets hang on these two commandments.'"

That's a high command, but one that the Church often forgets. I say all this, not to start a debate and not to judge the Church, as I am part of the fallible Church. I mention it to remind the Church that "the least of these" are sometimes right next door to us. Or under our own roofs.

There are many who are angry with the Church because of the hypocrisy they see in Christians. They must know that Jesus will never be unsure, hypocritical, or biased. Jesus will always help us hold that line, if we simply call on Him and let Him. When the agony is overwhelming, we can't do it ourselves. God gives us more than we can handle, but He doesn't give us more than He can handle.

Lastly, while the Church means well, they often don't know how to help. My encouragement to the Church is to start learning how to help these parents and children. Start asking questions, opening conversations, starting the dialogue. You don't have to be a wealthy institution to help, love, and support these parents. They need nights out, they need understanding, they need people to listen to them without judging them, and they need—above all things—lots of prayer.

Oftentimes, when the church recognizes a need, they ask the parents of children with special needs to start the program. These parents are exhausted, stressed, and not always gifted in the area of administration or organization. So, it's important to find individuals who are gifted and feel called to such a task so these parents can relax and enjoy a Sunday morning, knowing their children are taken care of and learning in an environment that suits them. There are plenty of churches that ARE creating these types of programs and they should be studied, modeled, and commended.

These parents are in a constant wilderness. They are enveloped in an overwhelming storm that never relents. We have to ask the question, "What would Jesus do?" and listen to the answer He provides. It sounds cliché, but it is the very question that needs to be asked every day.

I implore those who are reading this who don't have a child with special needs to remember . . . every Sunday you attend church, there are thousands of parents and children who are not there—not because they don't want to be, but because they simply can't attend because their children don't fit into that box. They feel isolated, alone, and as if they live on an island. They need you more than you can possibly know. Let's love more like Jesus. Let's change the narrative.

In Love,
Tiffany

# About the Author

Tiffany Haines continues to wrestle hurricanes alongside her family in North Carolina where she serves as a PANS family consultant. She also sits on the Board of Christian Family Life, a ministry whose mission is fueled by the truth that marriage matters. In her free time, she dreams of the day when PANS is no more, and we're all seated at the right hand of the Lord Almighty, in full understanding of the eternal weight of glory.

9 781631 953057